Advance Praise for *To Light Their Way*

Nothing brings you to your knees in prayer quite like becoming a parent. *To Light Their Way* is just that—a candle in the dark, a hand to hold, words to guide you when you have none. Kayla's warm, compassionate voice is a balm to weary parents everywhere, offering the perfect language to pray over a multitude of circumstances. This book has earned a permanent spot on my nightstand. I will be turning to these love-soaked prayers again and again as I raise my three children.

ASHLEE GADD
Founder of Coffee + Crumbs and author of *The Magic of Motherhood*

To Light Their Way is a beautiful invitation to pause and draw near to God, no matter the circumstance. For parents, this collection is a grace-filled place to turn when seeking language, hope, and peace.

MORGAN HARPER NICHOLS
Artist and poet

To Light Their Way is such an inspiring collection of liturgies and prayers that help families discuss and discern the themes of justice we want to see in our world. Kayla thoughtfully leads parents, children, and extended family down the path of truly living out Jesus' hope of seeing God's will be done on earth as it is in heaven.

JONATHAN "PASTAH J" BROOKS
Pastor; author of *Church Forsaken*

Few voices I've come across do the work of demystifying not only spiritual matters but also the sometimes overwhelming world of parenting. This book, like so much of Kayla's work, meets me in both places, providing pathways of language and imagery that help place me in my own secret and everyday life.

JUSTIN McROBERTS
Author of *It Is What You Make of It*

To live fully is to embrace the wonder of the ordinary and the mystery of God with us. These simple, meaningful prayers are a night-light, reminding us we are not alone. I will keep this beautiful book close at hand and reach for it again and again.

SHANNAN MARTIN
Author of *The Ministry of Ordinary Places* and *Falling Free*

Inspired, beautiful, heartfelt, compassionate, and real, these prayers will help you enter into a deeper relationship with God in almost every part of your life as a believer.

JAMES MARTIN, SJ
Author of *Learning to Pray*

As a mom to many foster children and one newborn baby, I have experienced the highest of highs and lowest of lows in my parenting journey. Moments with God are harder to come by when you have children whose needs demand all your time and attention. Time with God is essential for myself and my family. When I have time, I am often depleted and lacking the words to pray. Thankfully, Kayla Craig has provided this book full of beautifully woven prayers and liturgies for parents just like me. This is the book I didn't know I so desperately needed.

MANDA CARPENTER
Author of *Space: An Invitation to Create Sustainable Rhythms of Work, Play, and Rest*

Every parent or caregiver knows what it's like to stare down the hopes, fears, joys, and griefs of childrearing and struggle to find words to say, much less words to pray. This book is an expansive offering of grace, generously providing the language we all need to lift our children to the One who knit each and every one of them together in love.

SHANNON K. EVANS
Author of *Rewilding Motherhood: Your Path to an Empowered Feminine Spirituality*

These liturgies awaken us to the glory of children again and again. Kayla has curated a collection that is honest about every flawed and aching aspect of parenthood, yet her words are grounded in a deep gratitude for her role as keeper, protector, and lover of the little ones she calls her own. I suspect these prayers will be shared, remembered, and held close for many years to come.

COLE ARTHUR RILEY
Writer of *Black Liturgies*

To Light Their Way is a trusted companion for every parent's journey, honoring the bright and dark places along the way. Kayla Craig has given us a rich collection of liturgies to pray in quiet or proclaim together in chaos, a book for the joys and sorrows of raising children through milestone moments and mundane days. Kayla has a heart for justice, an ear for poetry, and clear eyes to see the world through grit and glory. Her prayers offer a deep breath and a drink of grace when we need it most. At the heart of each liturgy is gratitude for the goodness of family love, even when it is complicated or challenging. *To Light Their Way* is the prayer book so many of us have been searching for—strong in faith, wide in reach, and stubborn in hope.

LAURA KELLY FANUCCI
Author of *Everyday Sacrament: The Messy Grace of Parenting* and *To Bless Our Callings: Prayers, Poems, and Hymns to Celebrate Vocation*

Now more than ever, many of us are overwhelmed with the demands of parenting in such a loud world. With compassion, curiosity, and tenderness, Kayla Craig offers us sacred prayers and space for the complexity of parenthood. *To Light Their Way* is a gift to all of us who are seeking to stay rooted in faith as we navigate the beautiful and difficult terrain of raising kids.

AUNDI KOLBER
Licensed therapist and author of *Try Softer*

Breathtaking and transformational. This book takes us by the hand and shows us how to pray for our children through heartbreak and with a howl of hope in our chests. Don't miss this chance to light up milestones and meltdowns and everything in between with unflinching prayers of joy and generosity. We need more guides like Kayla in the world and on the bookshelf!

DIANA K. OESTREICH
Founder of the Waging Peace Project; author of Amazon's #1 new release in war and peace, *Waging Peace: One Soldier's Story of Putting Love First*

If written prayers are a light meant to help illuminate our path, *To Light Their Way* is a bonfire. When words won't come, when our groanings are all the communication we have, Kayla Craig has gathered hopes and laments like wildflowers, an overflowing basket of beauty to spur us onward. If you often find yourself stymied or overwhelmed by prayer, Kayla lets us borrow her hard-won words as she beckons us from just ahead on the road. *To Light Their Way* is honest, rich, and attentive to all the ways we can suffuse grace into our children's lives, as well as our own.

ERIN HICKS MOON
Host of the *Faith Adjacent* podcast; resident Bible scholar on *The Bible Binge* podcast; author of *Every Broken Thing, O Heavy Lightness,* and *Memento Mori*

Kayla Craig's stunningly beautiful gift of written word has, time and again, captured exactly what my spirit was longing to say in times of grief, celebration, and waiting. Her reflections in *To Light Their Way* will prove to do exactly this: they'll surely illuminate our spirits' longings as we hope for connection with the heart of God and one another. This collection is a holy offering from Kayla's heart to us—and I'm so grateful.

ASHLEE EILAND
Pastor, Mars Hill Bible Church; author of *Human(Kind)*

Simple and profound, gentle and bold, each page of *To Light Their Way* is packed with life. What a gift this book will be to all who find it. May it illuminate the paths of many. With this book, Kayla Craig has created something very special. It will be a source of hope and help for many years to come. In these pages, I saw reflected so many of the things I've often wanted to say but could not express. It's a reminder that we're not alone and that the aches and longings, joys and blessings of being a parent can lead us to a closer knowing of God's great, good love.

BRAD MONTAGUE
New York Times bestselling author of *Kid President's Guide to Being Awesome* and *Becoming Better Grownups*

In these days of nonstop parenting, I've been struck by how often I turn to one of Kayla's prayers. Though I have books and books on prayer, her words are fresh and yet familiar. They point me toward God, myself, and the people around me in love. Now that I get to work alongside Kayla, I'm all the more grateful for the deep well of prayer and love of both neighbor and Scripture that is evident in her life. Her words, work, and witness are a gift I can't wait to share with friends at baby showers and in the "I can't go on like this" moments.

JENN GILES KEMPER
Founder of Sacred Ordinary Days

A Collection of
Prayers & Liturgies for Parents

To Light Their Way

KAYLA CRAIG

TYNDALE
MOMENTUM®

The Tyndale nonfiction imprint

Visit Tyndale online at tyndale.com.

Visit Tyndale Momentum online at tyndalemomentum.com.

Visit the author at kaylacraig.com.

Tyndale, Tyndale's quill logo, *Tyndale Momentum*, and the Tyndale Momentum logo are registered trademarks of Tyndale House Ministries. Tyndale Momentum is the nonfiction imprint of Tyndale House Publishers, Carol Stream, Illinois.

To Light Their Way: A Collection of Prayers and Liturgies for Parents

Designed by Eva M. Winters

Edited by Stephanie Rische

Published in association with the literary agency of Books & Such Literary Management, 52 Mission Circle, Suite 122, PMB 170, Santa Rosa, CA 95409.

For information about special discounts for bulk purchases, please contact Tyndale House Publishers at csresponse@tyndale.com, or call 1-855-277-9400.

A catalog record for this book is available from the Library of Congress.

ISBN 978-1-4964-5400-3

Printed in China

27   26   25   24   23   22
7   6   5   4   3

To my children: May you know just how loved you are.
And to Jonny: It's my greatest joy to parent with you.

Contents

A Parade of Prayers

WHEN MY FAMILY GOES on walks together, we form quite the parade. Joseph speeds down the sidewalk on his scooter, leading the way, as eldest children often do. Asher isn't far behind him, pedaling furiously on his green bike, as Abram runs to catch up, sneakers illuminating the pavement. My husband rounds out the procession, pulling a worn red wagon, Eliza's very own chariot as we wait for insurance approval for a wheelchair. I linger behind, balancing two dogs' leashes in one hand and a mug of coffee in the other, marveling at my spot in this vibrant, wild, beautiful parade.

These walks, like family, like prayer, are a bit cobbled together, full of twists and turns. But they are filled with beauty and wonder nonetheless.

I marvel at the paths that brought us together—paths that weave through time and space, adoption and biology. As I parent these four children and journey with them through their wide range of ages and stages, I stand in awe of the image of God—the imago Dei—reflected in each heart and soul, mind and strength. I see their individual personalities break forth into the world, with their unique passions and frustrations, joys and heartbreaks.

When we get back from our neighborhood adventures, we turn the key and break through the door. Shoes become wayward heaps on the living room floor, sweaty kids and dogs gulp fresh water, and I collapse onto the couch, suddenly aware of my exhaustion. But every once in a while, when the windows are open and a breeze filters in, I become wide awake, aware of this gift of *together*. And though I can barely string words one after another, I offer a silent thank-you to God for each child that I've been given the privilege to parent.

moments, which begin in quiet and then are soon covered in the noise of a
g TV, shouting children, and at least one barking dog, I pray simple, integrated
prayers, asking God to breathe love into each child, to care for their varied needs, and to
light their way through each day.

Keeping It Simple

I'm aware of my propensity to overthink things, prayer included. Once a religious expert
stood up to test Jesus, asking what he must do to inherit eternal life. Jesus responded with
a question, as He often did: "What is written in the Law?" (Luke 10:26).

And the answer still stands, even in my cluttered and chaotic house, even now: "Love
the Lord your God with all your heart and with all your soul and with all your strength
and with all your mind." And the second part of it? "Love your neighbor as yourself"
(Luke 10:27).

So when I pray for each of my kids, I pray for their

heart,
soul,
strength (body), and
mind.

And I pray that in all things, they would know the love of God so deeply that they
would love themselves, and out of that would come an outpouring of love to the neighbor
down the road and the neighbor across the world.

When You Have No Words

Though I've been praying in some form or another since I was young, it took a critically ill
child to bring me to the rootedness of written prayers—or, as many traditions call them,
liturgies.

When a respiratory virus attacked my three-year-old daughter's lungs, she relied on a
ventilator to keep her alive. I sat by her too-big hospital bed, searching for reminders of
life as her sedated body struggled under the weight of drips and machines.

Three weeks in, I knew every nurse's name and every IV's purpose. My husband, Jonny,
and I were taking turns in the hospital, and that night he was home with our three young

sons. It was my night to sleep on the plastic pullout couch as the doctors and nurses came and went, checking stats and assessing numbers.

I couldn't hold my baby. I could barely even touch her head without disrupting her fragile body.

"Healing takes time," the doctors told me. "She's very sick. This is a life-threatening illness."

All I could do was sit under the fluorescent lights and wait. I wanted to pray but had not one ounce of energy to muster anything. And honestly, I wanted to yell at God. My heart raced; my face flushed. How could He let this precious child hang in the thin space between heaven and earth? Exhaustion flooded my bones. I was putting on a front for my boys at home, trading day and night shifts with my husband, and the schedule was taking its toll on my mind, body, and soul.

I looked outside as another blizzard blanketed the parking lot. I watched the minivans and sedans disappear under thick clouds of snow and wondered about the people each vehicle represented. Each car meant somebody's loved one was sick and in need of care. I thought of the suffering that people experience every day. I lamented. I doubted.

I wrestled with fears and doubts, and I wasn't sure if I could hand them over to God. I didn't know how. So instead, I held on to them. I couldn't hold my daughter. But I could embrace my anger and fear, clutching them close to my chest.

There I was, married to a pastor, and I couldn't pray.

There I was, a Christian for the previous thirty years, and I couldn't muster any words.

People told me they were praying for our little girl. *I guess your prayers don't work,* I thought. I knew that God wasn't a genie in a bottle who would just grant our wish if we all prayed hard enough. But still, I struggled to find words that rang true in the walls of that hospital room.

On one of my days at home, I checked the mailbox. Bills and junk mail spilled out, but there was a package nestled inside too. A book of prayers. There in my mailbox was an invitation into conversation with God—and permission to rest from the exhaustion of finding just the right words.

I didn't have to have it all together. I didn't have to have the perfect quiet space to center my thoughts—the beeps and buzzes of medical machines would do. All I had to do was open to the page and read, recite, and repeat until I felt my heart rate begin to calm, until I was no longer tensing my shoulders, until I could release the breaths I'd been holding for too long.

't need the perfect location or perfect circumstances or perfect words to pray. .. .or that, we never will.

When everything crumbled, the prayers of another voice comforted me. And as I prayed, the written words became my own pleas and petitions, jumping off the page and nestling into my soul. The warmth and welcome of the body of Christ says, *I'll lift your hands for you.* And as I learned in those thin spaces in the intensive care unit, the body of Christ also says: *You don't have the words? Here, take mine.*

After a month in the hospital, with the care of a compassionate crew of doctors and nurses, my husband and I brought our daughter home. I still didn't have any concrete answers about the mystery of prayer. I grieved for the parents who left the intensive care unit with empty seats in their minivans. I celebrated my daughter's return to health. I sat in the tension.

When we arrived home, unloading bag after bag of belongings, I clipped the plastic hospital ID bracelets from our wrists and tossed them into the trash. But I held on to the book. The prayers of others had become *my* prayers.

Likewise, may the prayers of lament and celebration in this book become yours.

They already are.

What Is Prayer?

Prayer isn't about selecting the most lyrical prose or saying a perfectly selected string of words. It's about entering into the ongoing dialogue the Creator of all things is *already* having with us every day.

When we weep at the grief circling our families, we pray.
When we lament the unjust headlines, we pray.
When we celebrate the joy, beauty, and love around us, we pray.
When we seek our rootedness in Christ alone, we pray.

God requires no sonnets or soliloquies—He just desires our presence. My four-year-old asked me recently if we can see God, and I told him we see God in the way a rainbow appears after a storm, we feel God in the way his sister cups her hand on my cheek, we hear God in the giggles of his brothers as they leap on the trampoline. Across cultures and generations, people have sought answers about how to interact with God. God requires no special sacrifice, demands no magic words or rituals. God just wants *us*.

Parenthood is sanctifying. It's often said that we do the best we can with what we have—and I believe a life that includes rhythms of prayer is part of that. Just like I call my mom after a particularly difficult day or after receiving exciting news, I can turn to God in my celebrations and sorrows—in the ordinary and extraordinary moments of life.

When we pray, we are transformed. We don't pray to a genie in a bottle but to the One who loves so extravagantly that He entered our reality and made a way to dwell inside us. Inside our blood, our sweat, our tears. He hears the rhythms of our hearts before we ever put words to them.

God isn't just present in the quiet mornings before the kids wake up or in the late nights on our knees. God is here among us, beyond all time and in all time.

As I raise my four kids, I marvel at their joys and sorrows, their glittering ability to see God's beauty in everything, even a dandelion-covered lawn. I ache for God's help as I tend to their hearts, minds, bodies, and souls, even as I'm unsure how to voice what's on my heart. Heavy headlines, packed schedules, the desire to raise kids in God's Kingdom—how can I possibly find the words to pray?

Fortunately, prayer doesn't have to be fancy. We don't have to have just the right words for God to listen. God is already listening. God is all around us, and holy moments live in the ordinary and extraordinary times in our lives.

Why Do We Pray?

We pray because we were created with a sense of awe and wonder, and we need a worthy outlet for those feelings. We pray because as children talk to their parents, so we talk with God. We pray because we ache to raise a generation that refuses to accept the world as it is but believes in a brighter reality rooted in peace and truth.

We pray because we're aware of our shortcomings and believe in a healing God who beckons us with open arms, no matter how far we've strayed. We pray for the inner child in our souls, the one who aches to return home.

We pray because we were made to. We pray because we love our children, and we believe they were knit together by a loving God who lavishes love upon generation after generation, who loves our children even more than we do and knows them better than we could even fathom.

We pray for our children, and in doing so, we know that we, too, will be transformed.

hat they would love the Lord their God with all their heart, soul, mind, and

We pray because if we ache for this transformation for our children, we know it starts with us. Through Jesus Christ, we receive supernatural nurture and cosmic grace. We pray because we need strength for the journey and reminders to rest along the way.

We pray that our children will love their neighbors as themselves. We pray that we will be bold enough to model solidarity with our oppressed neighbors because we know our children are watching. We pray that we will be tender enough to model gentleness to our children because we know our children are watching. We pray that we will be kind enough to care for the stranger because we know our children are watching.

What Are Liturgies?

Maybe you were raised in a tradition where prayer is spontaneous and free, never recited or rote, but you long for the roots that come from tradition and sacrament. Or maybe you have experienced liturgy as dry, dusty prayers written long ago, lacking relevance, emotion, or energy. Or perhaps prayer is something of a foreign concept to you—something that feels a little awkward and uncomfortable. In reality, liturgies are ecumenical—they go beyond denomination—and they don't require a spiritual résumé. Liturgies are a rhythm, a worship, rooted in God's Word.

Liturgies are written prayers that act as a sacred invitation into divine conversation with God. Jesus said that He left us the very Spirit of God, dwelling inside us. Through the Spirit, we can use liturgies as an on-ramp into an ongoing conversation with the Divine as we go about our days, rising in the morning, kissing skinned knees and helping with schoolwork, interacting with our neighbors, and finally resting our heads at night.

> Liturgies are threads that bind us together, weaving our tears and our laughter together.

Whatever tradition you grew up in or find yourself in (or don't find yourself in) now, the prayers in this book are reimagined liturgies that draw from the vibrant, varied fabrics of the broad Christian faith. I find comfort in the patchwork quilt of my own faith journey. When my Baptist grandmother married a Catholic, they raised a Lutheran daughter who married a Methodist and raised me Presbyterian. I fell in love with the son of a Baptist pastor and started to make my faith my own, feeling God sewn into the seams of modern church plants and old wooden pews, pulling the threads until I found myself back in the liturgical rhythms of my childhood.

Liturgy, the prayers of worship at times of celebration and lament, roots us in the ancient truth that God dwells in us and beside us. That we are called beloved and our children are called beloved, and that we are each a pebble in an ocean of deep, abiding love. Liturgy anchors us as the waves of real life wash over us. We pray in the mundane; we pray in the unknown; we pray when we have nothing left to give. Scripture tells us that the Spirit intercedes for us with wordless groans. God knows our ache. He sees us and will not leave us or our children.

I find deep comfort in knowing I'm not alone in my prayers—that others have prayed, are praying, and will pray these same words. Liturgies are threads that bind us together, weaving our tears and our laughter together. In liturgy, we're tied to our common humanity.

How to Use This Book

Henri Nouwen said that the key to praying is . . . well, praying.[1] Use these prayers in the morning before the chaos of the day begins. Or keep this collection on your bedside table, ready to flip open when your world is finally quiet. If you're like me, you'll have time to pray for five whole minutes while you wait in the carpool line or get stuck in a long commute.

Everything we have is a prayer—all we do, all we are. Prayer is a habit. And the more we practice entering into ongoing dialogue with God, the more we—and, in turn, our children and our very worlds—will be changed.

These prayers are modern liturgies, written with the love of God and neighbor embedded in every stanza. They're created to guide you into an intentional time of prayer for your children and the world they live in. These prayers are for parents who will not bury their heads in the sand during pain or suffering, because we know we are created and pursued by a God who is present in the pain. These prayers are for finding the sacred in the ordinary struggles and victories of raising children today. These liturgies are for the poor and the privileged, for those full of faith and those barely hanging on. Take comfort in knowing that though these prayers are deeply personal, they're also communal, read and recited by other parents across denomination and background.

This collection of prayers and liturgies is written from the perspective of a parent and sometimes from the communal perspective of a body of believers. An index in the back will help you find prayers by topic and theme.

Some liturgies, like the prayers for ordinary moments or prayers for nurturing faith and character, are general offerings you can pray daily. Others are for more specific situations. Pray them alone or with a partner, a friend, or a family member. Pray them at a church service or a baby shower or a birthday party.

These are prayers to celebrate birthdays and baptisms, as well as when your son stands alongside a bullied classmate or when your daughter tries something new, even when she's scared. These prayers are for when your child grieves the death of a grandparent or a goldfish, as well as lamenting the day your child comes home shaking because they had to participate in an active shooter drill at school.

You'll even find some prayers to pray along with your kids. The words in this book aren't meant to replace your quiet, everyday conversations with God but rather to help you when you could use a map on your journey. I've also found written prayers helpful for praying on behalf of a loved one walking through a certain joy or time of suffering, helping me grow in empathy and compassion for a situation I myself may not have personally experienced. You may find that you want to read some blessings over a child as a situation arises or find comfort in the solitude of reading them alone.

I should mention up front that this is not a book of cotton-candy prayers that ignore the raw realities we live in every day. Praying like that will rot our teeth. These are prayers to chew on. Prayers to pray when you're overwhelmed with emotion and when you feel nothing at all.

These words of lament and celebration, of the ordinary and extraordinary, reflect the joys and sorrows of generations of parents. These prayers and liturgies are rooted in the ancient truths of God's Word, big enough for all of us.

You'll also find a section of breath prayers inspired by Scripture. I've found these short meditations helpful to me as I go through the day. Whether I'm scrolling Twitter, loading the dishwasher, tackling a work project, or playing LEGOs with my kids, these are simple prayers to memorize. Simply pray the *inhale* words as you breathe in and pray the *exhale* words as you let your breath go. These simple meditations help root us in our bodies and souls, hearts and minds. They reset us to the Spirit of God, who is with us always, even when we forget that sacred truth. And bonus? These short prayers help us memorize Scripture. These breath prayers are simple, easy to remember (or jot down), and they can be helpful to pray with our kids, too.

All Shall Be Well

Parenting is challenging. This we know. May we accept the invitation to step into God's upside-down Kingdom, the now-and-not-yet, where the first will be last and where the little children are always welcome.

We move fast; these prayers help us slow down. Our worlds are loud; these prayers help us get quiet. Our children are full of wonder and mystery; these prayers help us grow in compassion for *all* of who our children are.

We pray because we need help. We pray because we stand in awe. We pray because we are grateful.

We pray because we are mothers and fathers. We are daughters and sons.
Let us pray.

Kayla Craig
Fall 2021

A Blessing to Begin

God, bless the hopes and anxieties,
The joys and the longings
Within us as we raise our children.

Bless the late nights
And the too-early mornings.
Bless the daily chaos
And the quiet moments, too.

Bless the growing hearts and souls
And their embodied hope.
Bless the future so full of promise,
And bless the past so full of grace.

Bless our belly laughs
And our bitter tears, too.
Bless the celebrations held
And the lessons hard won.

Bless the groans
When no words will form.
Bless the daily reshaping of our
     hearts
And the renewal of our minds
As we reshape and renew the world
With each act of love.

Bless the spirit inside us
That won't give up on Your love.

Romans 12:2

PART ONE

Prayers for Family Milestones

I'M NOT SURE HOW the *night before birthdays* has become such a thing in our family.

When we whisper the last bedtime story and tuck in the final covers, my husband and I sneak into the kitchen to blow up dollar-store balloons, balance on kitchen chairs to twist and hang streamers, and pull hidden gifts from under the bed. It's never fancy, and I often reuse birthday banners, but it always ignites a sense of anticipation. We're bone weary and brain exhausted in the throes of parenting four young children, but this ritual of coming together, of anticipating our kids' delight and surprise, builds excitement in our hearts.

We find ourselves reflecting on the day we met our birthday child—marveling at their growth, reflecting on what has been, and wondering what might be. The sprinkles I shake on the cupcakes become a prayer, and suddenly I'm remembering the moment I first laid eyes on them, praying over their spiritual journey in Christ. My searching for the last bit of Scotch tape to wrap a present is a prayer for their creativity and sticky fingers.

Celebration is a crucial tenet of the Christian life (see Philippians 4:4). We don't need grand parties or opulent gifts—even simple moments can serve as an invitation to remember, to enter into divine conversation and reflect on the joys of the complicated, curious humans we get to raise.

Parenting in times of celebration invites us into the present reality that the Spirit dwells among us. We know intimately that sorrows fill our lives, but the Christian life is also marked with much rejoicing, too. There are the big moments, of course, such as the birth of a child. But celebration also comes in the delighted squeal of a child at a new seedling sprouting from a cup of dirt or a flourishing touch on a finger painting or a teenager's first paycheck.

I'm inclined to focus on God and prayer when life is challenging. When I'm aware of my lack, I'm aware of my intimate need for God's provision and love. But when life feels celebratory, I'm likely to forget—to leave an invitation unsent for the Creator of all

1

good things, the Savior who sets the table (see Luke 22:14-16) and turns water into wine (see John 2:1-11). A Jesus who says take and eat (see Matthew 26:26). A God who is the orchestrator of the Year of Jubilee (see Leviticus 25:1-13).

When we pray for our children, when we mark our times of celebration, we're entering into the ancient tradition of worshiping a perfect God who is the very definition of parental love. These prayers of celebration include spiritual, developmental, and familial milestones—and also the small, sacred victories that are so easy to forget.

As parents, we need no reminder that our babies are worth celebrating. May we remember that this is how the Maker of all things feels about us, too—beloved simply because we are His children. Worthy of love simply because we *are*. And then may we accept this truth as a cause for celebration.

Living in celebration does not mean we wait until things are perfect to rejoice—it means we are aware of God's inherent goodness. We're awake to glimmers of extraordinary wonder in our comings and goings.

May these liturgies of milestones, family celebrations, and tiny victories remind us that we feast with God as we enter into the spiritual adventure of parenting and praying for our daughters and sons.

A Prayer for Pregnancy

You are the author of life, O God.
Through You all life is made.
Through Your wonder and Your love,
You are making all things new,
And we thank You
For the new life growing in the womb
    right now.

How is it possible, O God,
That You invite us into this wonder?
We pray for peace to flood our hearts
As we prepare to welcome
A new little one into our family.

As we hear the rhythm of the heartbeat,
Our hearts leap with anticipation
In expectation of what's to come.
Help us prepare to parent
And open wide our hearts
To love with abandon exactly who You
    created this baby to be.

We pray for a pregnancy rooted in health,
And if complications arise
With an unexpected change or diagnosis,
Help us to make life-honoring decisions
Rooted in love and not fear.
Surround us with supportive community,
And guide doctors, nurses, and midwives

As they walk us through these nine
    months.

As this baby grows and develops,
Dancing in the womb,
We praise You for the mystery of life
And the whispers of Your love
In the artistry of our intricate bodies.

As this child's brain forms in the womb,
We pray that they will
Love You with all their mind,
Growing in wisdom
And never hesitating to ask "Why?"
Or "Why not?"

As this child's heart grows in the womb,
We pray that they will
Love You with all their heart,
Growing in compassion
That overflows to everyone they meet.

As this child's eyes develop in the womb,
We pray that they will
Love You with all their soul,
Growing in mercy
To see the hurting and forgotten.

As this child's hands and feet sprout in
    the womb,
We pray that they will
Love You with all their strength,
Growing in gentleness,
Following Your paths of peace.

3

We pray for peace as bodies grow
    and shift
To make room.
Provide comfort of body
And soul.
Keep us focused on the anticipation,
And help us not to get distracted by
    nurseries we don't need
And parties with things we don't want.

As we trust in You,
May we also trust our bodies
In pregnancy, labor, and delivery.
In the groans, be near, O God.
In the pushes and pulls, be near, O God.
In the deep breaths and soaked brows,
    be near, O God.
Be near as we cry out to You.

Lord, we know that each baby born on
    this earth
Is Your beloved
And reflects Your image
In every eyelash fringe and fingerprint
    swirl.
And yet access to a safe birth
For mother and baby
Is not a reality for everyone.
We pray that You would make a way
For us to support
And advocate for mothers in our own
    community
And around the world
To have births that are

Safe, honoring, and dignifying,
Across every race and economic status.

In our worries, remind us to rest
In Your love that overflows
Like a mother nursing her baby.
Help us remember that You love this child
Because You are love,
And You love our sons and daughters
More than we ever could.
We pray that You would help us
Turn our pregnancy fears to You,
For You hold our children,
And even us,
In the very palm of Your hand.

Lord, help us trust the process of creation.
Thank You for the sacred gift
Of being cocreators with You.

Ecclesiastes 11:5; Ephesians 3:16-19; Psalm 139:13-14;
Isaiah 49:15-16

A Prayer
for Birth

O God, we pray for new life bursting
    forth—
For the first breath of a baby
And the tiny cries echoing through time
    and space.
O God, we pray for the moment skin
    meets skin—
For the exhales of a parent
And the loud cries echoing through time
    and space.
O God, this world groans like a laboring
    mother.
We need embodied hope, and we see a
    glimpse of it
In the pursed lips of a newborn,
In the tiny fingers and toes.

O Spirit, hover over this newborn life,
As You did in the womb.
Surround this beloved baby
With care and with comfort.
Surround this beloved family
With community and with courage.
Remind us that parenting is
A sacred offering of body and soul.
May love surround this baby and family
In all the stages of life,
In all the joys and the sorrows.

We pray this in the name of Jesus Christ,
Who entered our world through a
    mother.
We thank You for Your promise of hope
    everlasting.
We thank You for Your goodness and
    truth.

Remind us of Your heavenly nurture
And the human nature that You chose.
O God, may this child be bathed in
    Your light
And wrapped in the arms of Your love,
Today and forevermore.

Deuteronomy 32:11-12; Psalm 18:1-2; 1 Peter 1:3; James 1:17

O God, may
this child be
bathed in Your
light and wrapped
in the arms of Your
love, today and
forevermore.

A Prayer for Baptism

O God of Living Water,
We come to You on the day of this
    child's baptism
In celebration of Your promise,
In communion with Your people.

O Lord, we thank You
For the sacred act of baptism,
By grace alone.
As we watch the water droplets form
    and fall,
We remember Your story—
You, who created the universe
And made Your dwelling among us,
Living and dying and rising again.

Cleanse our hearts, O Lord,
As we pray for this child.
Refresh our spirits, O Lord,
As we pray for this child.

On this day, we see our reflection in
    the water
And affirm that through baptism in
    Jesus Christ,
We lay down our ways for Yours,
Forsaking the rhythms of the world
For the heartbeat of Your Kingdom.
Meet us in the water, O Lord.

Wash us with Your mercy.
May this moment in front of You
And Your people gathered
Mark a new beginning
Of a life set apart and made new.

O Christ, You entered our world
And conquered death
For the sake of this child.
May we love this little one
As You first loved us.

We thank You for Your covenant love
That flows like a mighty river.
We gather as an act of faith
And in celebration of Your faithfulness.

May [child's name]'s steps lead back
    to You.
Reveal Yourself in each person
They meet along the way.
We pray that Your great love
Will overflow in our family.
We pray that Your Holy Spirit
Will pour out in
The sisterhood and brotherhood of
    believers.

May this time seal in our hearts
A celebration of what You have done
And will do.
Be with us as this baptism marks
    a preparation
For the work of Your Spirit.

May this water and this child
Act as a visual reminder
That [child's name] belongs to You.
Be their ever-present fount
Of refreshment and renewal.

May every baptism remind us
Of our own spiritual journey,
And whisper into our hearts
Our own spiritual identity.
May we be reminded of what
Our parents or church families
May have prayed over us
As the water covered us.
Over and over again,
May we be pressed into mission
By our baptismal identity.

Lord, we pray that this child
Will know they are covered by
    the water
Of Your grace and truth.
May they have a spiritual memory
Of a foundation rooted in faith
Through Jesus Christ.
May they feel in their very soul
Love from a well that won't run dry.

On the day of this baptism,
We thank You for Your presence
In us and among us.
Go before [child's name],
And when they have the choice,
May they always choose love.

We pray that these baptismal prayers
Will remind us that we belong to
    each other
And to You, O Lord.
We pray for this baptism
In the name of the Father
And of the Son
And of the Holy Spirit,
Amen.

_____

Ephesians 4:4-6; Acts 2:39; Galatians 3:27-28

A Prayer for Baby Dedication

O God, we thank You for the arrival
    of [child's name].
On this day,
We dedicate this beloved child to You.
We stand before a community of believers
And before Your throne,
And as we hold this baby,
We pray that they would know they
    are loved
Deeply and unconditionally
By their family
And by You, O Lord.

May this little one grow to walk in paths
    of peace,
Run the race set out before them,
And lie down in Your green pastures
When they're tired, O Lord.
May this child grow in truth and in
    gentleness,
In wisdom and in grace.
May this child dance with abandon
And never be afraid to cry.
May they be rooted in love
And live with open hands and heart.

Help us raise this child
To choose peace over violence

And empathy over judgment.
Give us the gift of community
Anchored in Your love.
Give us the gift of others
Who will act as a compass
When we need Your help
Or when our child has lost their way.
May they follow You
And proclaim the miracle of who
    You are
In all they create,
In all they say,
In all they do.

We thank You for the gift and privilege
Of raising this child
And ask for Your help
As we journey through this life
    together.
Guide us like a star in the sky;
Illuminate the way
So we can parent [child's name]
With the mercy and grace
That comes from You and You alone.

We commit to raising this child to
    know You
As the living God.
We know that in You, all are given life.
You have created this child in love,
And we commit to raising them in
    that love,
Surrounded by the body of Christ.

Thank You for [child's name].
Thank You for our family.
And thank You for our sisters and
    brothers in Christ.

We pray this in Jesus' name,
Amen.

———————————

Hebrews 12:1-3; Psalm 23:2; Ephesians 2:10; Isaiah 44:24

May this child dance
with abandon and
never be afraid
to cry. May they
be rooted in love
and live with open
hands and heart.

A Prayer for a Child's Birthday

O God, Creator of time
And Creator of us,
For this child we pray.

We remember the day
We welcomed them into our hearts,
The way they felt in our arms,
And how life together fell into place just so.

O God, we light the candles,
Our faces aglow around the table,
And we sing together,
Joining in a melody of memories
And hopes for the future.

For this child we pray
That as the years go by, they will know
They are loved and wanted and treasured
Just as You made them.
May they feel secure in their place in
    the world,
And as their body and mind grow,
Whisper in their heart Your great love.

We look at the carousel of snapshots
Held tightly in our hands
And ache for our babies to be ours forever.
But we know, Lord,
That while we love in a way only
    a parent can,

Deeper and wider than we ever dreamed,
Our children are not ours at all.
They are Yours, Lord,
And Yours alone.

In the coming year,
May our child feel the sun upon their face,
And may they know what it is to sit in
    the dark
So that they may grow in wisdom.
May they wipe the sweat of justice from
    their brow,
And may they know what it is to ask
    forgiveness
So that they may grow in mercy.
May they be surrounded by kindness
    and gentleness,
And may they know what it is to be
    patient
So they may grow in grace for others.

O God, on this birthday,
Bless and keep this child.
May they always hold the wonder of
    youth within their soul.
May they always grow more into the
    person
You've created them to be.
May they walk in Your goodness
And stand in Your truth.
May they feel the love that swirls all
    around them
And hangs in the air and fills their lungs
As they close their eyes to make a wish.

For this child we pray:
Be with them as they embark
On the adventure of the coming year.
Grant them holy mischief and sacred
    shenanigans,
And permit them to rest.
When they stumble,
May they know Your healing touch.
Be with them as they enter new chapters,
And when they feel their story taking an
    unexpected turn,
May they know that You never stop
    writing.

For this child we pray
And ask that You would go before them
So that goodness and mercy
Will follow them all the days of their life.

Luke 10:30-37; Ephesians 6:10-18; Psalm 23:6

O God, we light the candles, our faces aglow around the table, and we sing together, joining in a melody of memories and hopes for the future.

We look at
the carousel
of snapshots
held tightly
in our hands
and ache for
our babies
to be ours
forever.

A Prayer for a Sibling Preparing for a New Baby

O God, as we prepare
To bring a new life into this world,
We acknowledge that this beginning
Marks the end of a chapter
In our family.
So we take this time
To thank You
For the memories we have shared.

And, too, Lord,
We look ahead with anticipation
For the memories waiting to be made.
We pray for sibling bonds
To be formed through Your love
That knits stories together.
As [child's name] becomes a new
    [brother/sister],
We pray they will know deep in their soul
That a parent's love multiplies
And never subtracts.

As we expect a new baby,
We ask for new ways to make our family
    as it is now
Feel seen and known and treasured.
As nurseries are painted,
We pray You would make room
In the hearts of our children.

Will You whisper a sense of wonder,
Of joy and anticipation?
Thank You for the gift of family,
Of time that slips away
Until we're forced to reckon
With its passing beneath our feet.
Surround this growing family
With Your great love.

_____

Mark 9:36-37

13

A Prayer for Adoption

O God, thank You for weaving stories
Of love and of loss
Into a tapestry
Big enough to wrap ourselves in.

For this child we pray,
That we would honor the complexities
Of what it means to be adopted.
We pray that we will hold space
For joy and for grief,
For tears and for laughter.

Guide our steps as we enter into this
    covenant
Of family,
Of stories held together
By threads of love,
By three-stranded cords.
Make us strong in the stories
Of birth family,
Adoptive family,
And adoptee.

May this child know that they are beloved
And that they can always take refuge
Under this broad quilt of all they are
And all who cherish and love them.

In our parenting,
Give us openness to tell the truth with care.

Give us humility for what we can never
    understand.
Give us grace in our connections and
    bonds.
May we instill confidence,
And may we protect and cherish
The fabric of our child's past.
May we guide them as they create
The beauty of their future.

In You, kinship is broader than we can
    imagine.
In You, family includes bloodlines
And goes beyond it too.

In our shortcomings,
Help us humble ourselves to listen
And learn.

O Lord, we see the glory of this child
In all they are
And in all You are.
We pray that we will honor
The privilege of doing life together
As parents and children
Under the blanket
Of Your love.

Romans 15:13; Ecclesiastes 4:12

14

A Prayer for When a Child Shares Good News

God of joy, thank You
For this child and the bounce in their step
And the pride in their eyes
As they recount good news from
    their day.
Help us remember the unfettered joy
    of youth
And the happiness that comes
In rejoicing together.

Thank You for the victories,
Big and small,
For the celebrations
Of a fear conquered
Or a friend made.

Thank You for good gifts
Of high-fives and fist bumps,
Of laughter and squeals of joy.
For we are an Easter people,
Eager to celebrate.

Help us never to be so lost
In our own realities that we are too busy
To enter into the joys of childhood.

May our children know just how worthy
They are of praise,

And may they never feel too self-conscious
To invite others into their good news.

O God who turns water into wine,
We know You are a God of celebration,
And we thank You for the gift
Of celebrating with our children.
For though their big news is their own,
The gift of parenthood is an open door
Into a shared celebration.

Thank You, Giver of good gifts.
Help this child see Your glory,
Your goodness, and Your love
In this moment—and give them also
A heart for those who may be hurting
    right now.
As we celebrate,
Stoke the fires of compassion and empathy.
Remind us that laughter is
A holy resistance to the suffering of the
    world.
Thank You for the special ways
You have created our children.
Help them see You in each celebration
And in every time of sorrow.
Give us eyes to see the good
And hearts eager to celebrate.

Let us always invite more to the table.
Let us cultivate confident hearts and
    courageous souls.
Let us celebrate!
May we never be too distracted

To celebrate with our children
For earning a high mark,
For accomplishing a big task,
For creating a piece of art,
For trying something new.

We know behind every victory
Are a million unseen pieces
Coming together in this moment.

Thank You for our children.
In a world that seems covered in heartbreak,
These little ones remind us to celebrate.

Thank You for their tender hearts
And the delight they cultivate
With their joyful spirits.

Create a celebratory spirit in us, O Lord.
Give us space in the day
And in our hearts
And in our minds
To rejoice!
To dance!
To let the heaviness of the world rest.

Your burden is light,
And we rest in the celebrations,
Big and small.

Let us learn from the uninhibited joy of
    children.
In their exuberance, may we see ourselves.
May we speak life into our little ones
So that they may know their worth
And be able to call out the good in others.

May they never feel like their productivity
Determines their worth,
And may they always know they are
    worth celebrating
Simply because they are.

We know that victories vary
From child to child,
From season to season.
We ask for eyes to see them
And hearts eager to lift them up
And spin them around until we're dizzy
With glad hearts and joyful spirits.

Thank You for this gift of parenthood.
May we remember Your abundant
    goodness
And shout joyfully of Your righteousness.
May this help us remember
The good news of Jesus Christ,
The good news always worth celebrating.

Psalm 126:3; Psalm 145:7; Isaiah 61:1-3

The gift of
parenthood is
an open door
into a shared
celebration.

16

A Prayer Before Leaving on Vacation

As we pack our bags and plot adventures,
We come to You, O God of all things,
And ask You to lead us in our travels.

Thank You for the energy and
    excitement
Of embarking on a new journey,
Whether we're exploring our hometown
Or setting sail to faraway places.
Ignite in us a childlike anticipation
Of what's to come.
Breathe in us the magic
Of being too excited to sleep.

Thank You for the wonder and whimsy
Of watching our kids fill their backpacks
With stuffed animals and books,
With sustenance for the journey.
Thank You for the great escape
Into time together.

Thank You for memories we will make,
For snapshots strung together in time
Like photographs on a postcard.

O God, help us to be present,
To have eyes to see the beauty
In the family right in front of us.
Help us to look more at each other
And less at our screens.

Thank You for the natural wonders
You've breathed into existence—
For the mountains and beaches
And wide-open spaces,
And for cities and the people in
    them too.

Thank You for souvenir shops
And unexpected pit stops,
For travel-size shampoo bottles
And well-worn maps,
For the airplane pretzels
And the sandwiches packed in the cooler,
For campsites and hotel beds.

As we prepare for this vacation,
Release us from the baggage
Of grown-up worries,
And let us linger in the fun
Of a getaway together,
For we know it is less about
Where we go
And more about who we're with.

Thank You for a little extra
In our wallet to make this adventure
    come true,
And we pray that we would remember
Those who do not have the privilege
Of money or health or time
To take a trip away.
Help us to be generous with our
    neighbor
As You are generous with us.

Be with us as we depart, O God.
And if we get lost, give us at least a
    good story
That our kids will tell and tell again.
Help us to be kind to those we meet along
    the way.
May they know us by our kindness and
    glad spirits.

Proverbs 3:5-6; Psalm 23:6; John 13:35

O God, help us
to be present,
to have eyes to
see the beauty in
the family right
in front of us.

A Prayer to Welcome a New Pet

O Maker of heaven and earth,
Thank You for the good gift
Of a new pet in our home.

You are the God who makes
The dragonfly
And the goldfish,
The calico kitten
And the wrinkled bulldog.

You call them by name,
The creatures You've made—
The fish of the sea
And the birds of the sky.
And just as You let us
Name all Your creatures,
We get to name this little companion
That we welcome into our family.

We marvel at Your creation,
The creatures that reflect
The wonder and whimsy
Of You.
In the caring for this creature,
May we catch glimpses of Your love
In new ways.

Help our children to grow
As they nurture this new family member.

As we care for [pet's name],
Help us to be gentle.
Help us to love
And to receive love in return.

Thank You for furry companions
And for the scaly friends in their tanks.
Thank You for the laughs
And for another living thing to share
    our lives with.
Thank You for their cuddles
And for their quirky charm.

Thank You for animals
And for giving us the chance to care
    for them.
May we be delighted by the ways they
    fill a spot
We didn't even know existed
In our human hearts.

May this pet be well cared for.
Ignite in our children a sense of
    responsibility
And duty to their fellow creatures.
We thank You for the opportunity
To care for [pet's name].
May it find warmth
In the little hands and hearts
That are eager to welcome it into our
    family.

Watch over us as we make memories
And marvel at our children,

Who never stop surprising us
In how they learn to love in new ways,
In how they learn to love
Outside of themselves.

In the melody of a bird chirping,
In a dog barking,
We recognize the privilege of caring for
    a pet
When many of our brothers and sisters
Live with so much want.

May our pet remind us to be generous
With our hands
And with our hearts.
Amen.

Genesis 1:20-25; Isaiah 11:6-9

PRAYER TO PRAY WITH CHILDREN

O God, You have made all animals—
Dogs and cats, birds and snakes,
Bunnies and fish—You made them all!
Thank You for [pet's name].
Help us show love and make a special
    space
In our hearts and our home for our
    new pet.
Help us show care.
We know that we can love
Because You first loved us.
Amen.

1 John 4:19

PART TWO

Prayers for Ordinary Moments

THE CURIOSITY AND CARE my children bring to our evening walks amaze me. Our neighborhood has wooded paths that twist and turn behind our 1970s split-level houses. While I check my watch to measure my heart rate and my steps, my preschooler marvels over the wild blackberries, delights in the vibrant hues of the setting sun, and lingers near the noisy woodpecker in the tree. His older brothers have a keen sense for spotting the sleeping deer I never would have noticed. They have the spiritual eyes to see the wonder in the ordinary.

What's a regular walk to me is a wilderness journey to them. As we forge along the paths, they skip ahead and shout out what they see, reminding me of God's goodness, of God's promise never to leave us or forsake us (see Deuteronomy 31:6). I find myself asking God to give me the perceptiveness of a child so that I might feel the Spirit in my everyday comings and goings.

Paula D'Arcy puts it this way: "God comes to us disguised as our life."[2] She experienced God's love in the depths of grief—her husband and one-year-old child died in a car accident when Paula was three months pregnant—and she has spent her life ever since writing about God's presence in our everyday realities.

In times of sorrow, like a funeral, or in times of celebration, like a wedding, we often remember to pray as we mark the significant moments of life. But when it comes to the ordinary rhythms and routines of everyday parenting—packing lunches, rushing out the door in the morning, helping with homework—it's easy to get caught up in the next thing on the agenda. It's easy to lose sight of the sacred invitations God gives us in the smallness of our lives.

Changing a diaper, mixing cookie dough, fixing a flat tire—all of these can be opportunities for prayer stitched into the fabric of life together.

In our prayers for everyday victories and defeats, we quiet our hearts and center ourselves in the present. It's often said that our children will change the world *someday,* and as adults, we can get lost in this future thinking. We ask sticky preschoolers what they want to be when they grow up and inquire what broody teenagers will study in college. (I admit, there's a "future freedom fighter" shirt hanging in my son's closet.) But when we get lost in this language, we miss out on God's image in our children *right now*; we gloss over God's reflection in the daily rhythms of life.

Our children reflect the very image of God, and it's a gift to be fully with them in the present, not because of who or what they may be in the future. I want to raise children who are awake to the world around them and to the needs of their neighbors. I want to be intentional in acknowledging the ordinary moments of our lives, because who my children are—who our family is—matters right now. Our children's stories don't start the moment they turn eighteen; God began writing the chapters of their lives way before we can even imagine (see Genesis 15:5).

As a parent to a child with significant disabilities, I have become keenly aware of the celebration of the small things, the sacredness of the quiet moments, and the power of staying in the present. Parenting a child who is dependent on my care, who may never hit the milestones of her typically developing peers, has reminded me of the importance of *right now* (see Matthew 6:34). We are called beloved simply because we are God's children. God's love is not contingent on what we do or what we achieve—and the same is true for our children.

God's delight doesn't require anything of us, which is countercultural to our production-focused, output-required ways of thinking. We have a God who delights in the small things. We see God's love in the beauty of today, in the vision of what is. When we begin to see parenting as a holy circle instead of a rigid line, our prayers become so much more than bargaining with God, so much fuller than the "if, then" statements.

In the liturgical calendar of the Christian church (see the appendix on page 205–206), half of the year is called "Ordinary Time." It's the space after Easter and before Advent, when there aren't major holy days. As a parent, I often feel that time inches by, and then all at once, I'm scrolling on my phone late at night, lost in photo albums of soft cheeks and squishy rolls of my son who is now almost taller than me. So much of our lives happen in these seemingly ordinary moments. If only we could see them as extraordinary.

May these prayers put words to the small yet sacred moments of life together, reminding us that God is in all things (see Colossians 1:17).

A Prayer for Mercy in the Mundane

We thank You for the unmade beds
And pray for those without a soft and
safe place to land.
We thank You for toothpaste on the
bathroom mirror
And pray for those who ache for someone
to share their life with.

We thank You for the fruit flies in the
kitchen
And pray for those whose hands pick the
produce we take for granted.
We thank You for the cool air pumping
through the house
And pray for those working tirelessly,
wiping sweat from their brow.

We thank You for the piles of dirty clothes
growing in the laundry room
And pray for those who collect coins for
the laundromat.
We thank You for the fits of summer
boredom
And pray for those whose tired minds and
bodies ache for the chance to rest.

Lord, in our desire to raise rooted
children,
We have lost ourselves to right theories
and theologies,

Believing that saying the right thing is the
same as doing the right thing.
We have rested comfortably in our
privilege,
Falling into ordinary rhythms and
routines
That focus on our family and forget our
neighbor.

Lead us in our understanding of
mutuality,
And open our eyes and hearts
So we may love inside and outside of
our homes.

Psalm 9:1; Romans 13:10; John 15:12

23

A Prayer for Feeding a Baby

O God who does not forget us,
Help me remember You are near
In the sleepless nights,
The midnight feedings,
And the too-early mornings.

Help me remember You are near
In the warmed-up bottles and stained
     nursing tanks,
In the rocking chairs and swaddling
     blankets,
In the burp rags and the diaper blowouts,
In the undereye bags and the reheated
     coffee.
I am bleary-eyed
And so in love
As I marvel at this little creature,
Whom I get to call my child.

Help me remember You are near
As I feed my footie-clad babe
At my breast or with a bottle
Or with the help of a feeding tube.
Thank You for the beautiful ways
Parents can provide nourishment
To help our babies grow.

Help me remember You are near.
Thank You for the connection

And magic that happens skin to skin,
For the eye contact that nurtures
     bonding,
And for the way that little hand
With tiny fingers
Reaches up
And pulls on my heartstrings just so.

Help me remember You are near
In these moments that tick by.
They say the years are short,
But I know too well the nights are long.
In the moments when my patience
     is thin
And my capacity is stretched,
Extend Your peace like a river
And Your glory over everything like an
     overflowing stream.

Help me remember You are near
As I sway and rock my child to sleep.
May I remember You are the Rock
     of ages—
Like a loving parent who doesn't
     abandon
But rather promises care,
Like a mother who nurses a baby
And carries her little ones on her hip.

Help me remember You are near.
In my fears and hopes for my baby—
Who they may be
And what they may be like—
Comfort me.

As a mother and father soothe their child,
You give compassion even greater than
    any human bond.

Help me remember You are near.
It's amazing to us, God,
That You love our babies more than
    we do.
Thank You for the gift of caring for them
And feeding them.
Will You nourish their minds and bodies,
    hearts and souls?
Will You nourish us, too?

Help me remember You are near
To the mothers and fathers
Who can't feed their babies
The way they would if they could
And must make impossible decisions
    to survive
And keep their babies full.
I pray that You will move within me
A spirit of compassion
To work for a more just world
So that all babies may eat.
Help me live with open hands
So that other parents may have the
    dignity
Of feeding their little ones
By their own hands.
Help me remember You are near.
Help me not forget these moments,
For this fleeting time
Will be so easy to forget.

For formula, we give thanks.
For the milk of a mother, we give thanks.
For bottles, we give thanks.
For the breast, we give thanks.
For babies to nourish, we give thanks.
For a world in which they'll flourish,
    we give thanks.

_____

Isaiah 26:4; Colossians 2:6-7

A Prayer for a Meal Together

O Jesus Christ, who says take, eat,
And do this in remembrance of Me,
We give thanks
For the gift of Your presence
And the gift of gathering at the table,
Sharing in our humanity and breaking
    bread
In the sacred space of together.
At worn wooden tables
Or tiny kitchen islands
Or trays in front of the TV,
We give thanks.

For access to abundance
And the hands that farmed each field
And picked each fruit and each vegetable,
We give thanks.
For clean water to scrub the dirt away,
For soil that helps good things grow,
And for sun that shines its face upon
    the earth,
Revealing Your glory,
We give thanks.

For the growing bodies and minds
Gathered around the table,
Hungry to be nourished and nurtured,
Never knowing what it's like to have
    hunger pangs,
We give thanks.

For the cupboards full of breads and boxes,
Cans and containers,
For the cool refuge of a stocked
    refrigerator,
We give thanks.

For the chopping and the stirring,
For the measuring and the baking,
For the eager hands that make more mess
    than not,
We give thanks.
For the stained cookbooks with smudged
    pages,
For the lingering aromas dancing in
    the air,
For the meals that turn out nothing
    like the blog said,
We give thanks.

For the frozen chicken nuggets
And the bakery-fresh donuts,
For the boxed macaroni and cheese
And the backyard tomatoes,
We give thanks.
For the crust-off sandwiches,
For the grapes sliced four ways,
For the squeezed juice boxes,
And the accidental milk spills—
We give thanks for these, too.

For the spirited discussions,
For the exasperated sighs,
For the dramatic eye rolls,
And for the monosyllable answers,
We give thanks.

For the kitchen sink full of dishes,
For the cluttered counters,
For the table littered with crumbs,
For the floors waiting to be swept,
We give thanks.
For hands that are plunged into warm
    water,
Slipping into the routine of the holy
    ordinary
Of soap and bubbles
And "You wash; I'll dry,"
We give thanks.

As we eat with our family,
May we throw open doors
To share our food with our neighbor,
For what is ours is really Yours.
May we be mindful of the foods we
    purchase
And how the choices in our cart affect
    another.
May we remember those who work
    long hours,
Stocking shelves or tending fields,
For their fingerprints line our
    shelves.
May we give out of what we have,
Even if it's just a few loaves and
    a few fish,
For You desire for all to eat,
And we need not hoard
Our daily bread.
For this, we give thanks.

In all we prepare
In times of harvest
And times of lack,
May we remember
That we belong to one another,
Connected by our mutual need
For the Bread and Wine
That feeds our souls.
We give thanks for all these things
In the name of Jesus Christ our Lord,
Amen.

_____

Matthew 26:26-29; John 6:1-14

As we eat with our
family, may we
throw open doors
to share our food
with our neighbor,
for what is ours is
really Yours.

A Prayer for a Weekend at Home

You are a God who creates
And a God who rests.

In the midst of
Babies sobbing,
Soothe us;
Children scrambling,
Settle us;
And teenagers sulking,
Sustain us.

Breathe life into dry bones
So we may know what it is to create.
Beckon us to lie down
So we may know what it is to rest.

We thank You for this time together
And pray for mothers and fathers,
Grandparents and caregivers
Who spend the weekend working,
Hour by hour,
To fill cupboards for their children.
For theirs is the Kingdom too.

May the memories we make
And the time we spend together
In prayer and at work,
In rest and at play,
Fuel us for the week ahead.

Psalm 62:5; Galatians 6:2; Luke 18:16

A Prayer for When You're Apart

O God of all things, big and small,
Thank You for looking after us
In our comings and goings.
Though we may not be together
    right now,
We know that You go before us,
Guiding us and leading us as we start
    each new day.

Thank You for creating a love
So big between us,
Parent and child,
That we have the holy ache
Of missing each other.

When my child is sad,
May You comfort them in their sorrow
And bring someone to wipe their tears
When I cannot.
When they are joyful,
May You be near in their rejoicing
And bring someone to celebrate with them
When I cannot.
When they are afraid,
May You guide them through their fear
And bring someone to soothe them
When I cannot.
Bring us back to each other full of heart,
Brimming with stories and adventures
To share with each other.

Until we meet again,
Help us to focus on
Where You've placed us for the day.
Help us center in on
Who and how You would have us love
On this day.

O Creator of time and place,
You are a God big enough to hold
Every tiny detail of our lives,
And we know You are big enough to be
    with us now,
Both parent and child,
As we are apart.

Comfort my child when they are afraid,
And give me the strength to hand my
    desire for control
Over to You.

Help me to remember that You alone
    are God.
And while You have entrusted this child
    to me,
They are Yours and Yours alone.

Thank You for the gift of communication.
Though we may be apart,
We can see each other through a screen.
But we know these replacements can
    never measure up
To the warm embrace of *together*.

When my child awakes to a new day,
May they do so surrounded by love.

And when they look up to the moon
   at night,
May they do so knowing they're held
By the One who hung the stars.

Bring us safely together soon.
With bated breath, we anticipate our
   reunion.
But until we can be with each other again,
Thank You for the gift of missing
   each other,
For that means we have loved
And have known what it is to be loved.
And as we are apart,
We pray for the children and parents
Who by no fault of their own
Have been separated from each other.

God, grant them supernatural peace
As they ache for each other.
May an invisible thread tie them together
In Your great love.
Give comfort to the lonely;
Give hope to the brokenhearted;
Give peace to the sorrowful.
We know this world isn't as it should be,
And we pray that we may work for a day
When mothers and fathers,
Daughters and sons
Will embrace each other
And wipe away one another's tears
And be united in
Heart and mind,
Body and soul.

As I am apart from my child,
I pray that You would
Embrace their heart with Your warmth
So that they may love those in their path.
Encourage their soul with Your grace
So that they may dwell in Your spirit.
Inspire their mind with Your brilliance
So that they may know You in all they
   encounter.
Ignite their strength with Your power
So that they may live with courage and
   compassion.

We can't wait to be together again,
And yet You have put us on diverging
   paths.
So give us strength for the journey,
And lead us back together again soon.
Though we miss each other,
We know we are not alone,
For You have surrounded us
With Your everlasting love.
Amen.

Psalm 121:7-8; Job 9:9

When my child awakes
to a new day,
may they do so
surrounded by love.
And when they look up
to the moon at night,
may they do so
knowing they're held
by the One who
hung the stars.

A Prayer for When Your Child Is Sick at Home

To the Maker of all things bright and
    beautiful,
To the Creator of all bodies,
Small and vulnerable,
May You present Yourself
In every nose wiped,
Temperature checked,
And blanket touched.

In their warm foreheads,
Give them rest.

In the tissues crumpled on the floor,
Give us hope.

Let us remember
You are the God who sees,
Who makes good bodies.

In every jagged breath and
Every fever dream,
May we remember that
We nurture our children because
You have shown us
Divine love.

For disrupted schedules
And reminders of
Our shared humanity,
We turn to You—
You, the God who never abandons
In the aches
And exhaustion
Of sickness
And of caring for it.

Give us rest
In the form of
Soft pillows
And community support.

For the clean water on the nightstand,
We give thanks.
For the doctor on call,
We give thanks.
For the pharmacy window,
We give thanks.
And we pray for the day all parents
Can have access to sick days
And bedside care.

Give healing to the weary
In our home
And around the world.

We pray this in the name of Jesus,
Who did not shirk humanity

Or imperfect immune systems,
Who knows intimately and infinitely
Our children's congestion
And our own human condition.

We pray this in the name of Jesus,
Who was cared for
By His earthly parents
And by You.
Amen.

───────────

Philippians 2:7; John 1:14

In every jagged breath
and every fever dream,
may we remember that
we nurture our children
because You have
shown us divine love.

A Prayer for a Stressful Morning

We so often forget,
In our own stress and struggles,
That children, too,
Find their brains and bodies
Flooded with the pulsing
Rush of worry.

Help us embrace our children
With a sense of compassion,
Of understanding,
Of patience,
And of peace,
Just as You do with us.

In times when we
Don't understand
And even express anger at
A son's shout
Or a daughter's refusal,
We acknowledge our lack.
We recognize our need
For help.

We thank You for the rush
Of a busy morning,
For that means we have
The gift of community
Woven into our very home.

With the spilled oatmeal and
A half-eaten banana,
Remind us of our abundance
Of food purchased, food transported.
We think of the cashier at the
    grocery store
And the field worker who picked
    the banana,
And we thank You for the hands
    that touched
What fills our cupboards,
Knowing many, too, are parents,
Waking at dawn,
Feeding children,
And doing their best.

We acknowledge the privilege
Of getting frustrated
At a child losing her left shoe
In a sea of sandals and boots,
For we don't even know who made the
Many shoes we wear.
We don't even know how many
Parents ache to give their children
Just a sliver of our abundance.

Thank You for the good gift
Of mounting dirty dishes,
For we have clean water
And hands to rinse them.

Thank You for the good gift
Of a pouting child,

And a sulking teenager,
For they have emotions,
And emotions tell us how we feel.

Thank You for the good gift
Of a ticking clock,
For You have given us time,
And we are living out memories together.

We marvel at the growing
Hearts and minds
And bodies and souls
We care for,
And we give this morning
Back to You.

Thank You for Your mercy
And unfailing love
In this seemingly mundane
And muddled morning.

We sense Your Spirit
Even now,
In the hive of activity,
In the exhaustion of a day
That has barely begun.

Be with us as we stay
And as we go.
You are with us in the
Backpacks and hats;
You are with us in the
Packed lunches and
Travel coffee mugs.

Give us eyes to see You
In everyone we will meet today,
And bring us home
With joy in our steps,
Marveling at Your wonder
And care for Your children.
Amen.

_____

James 3:17-18; 1 Thessalonians 5:16-18; Lamentations 3:22-23

A Prayer for Playing Together

Spirit, ignite in us the gift of creativity.
Let us enter into the mess-making,
For in the markers and paints and
    paper scraps,
We experience You in new ways.

Spirit, spark in us the gift of adventure.
Let us enter into the exploration of new
    kingdoms,
For in the slaying of dragons and the
    meeting of fairies,
We see Your wonder.

Spirit, breathe in us the gift of
    imagination.
Let us enter into the building of sacred
    spaces,
For in the blanket forts and secret
    passages,
We feel Your shelter.

Spirit, illuminate in us the gift of
    expression.
Let us enter into the song and dance of
    our youth,
For in the symphonies of childhood,
We hear Your glory.

In Your wonder, in Your shelter,
    in Your glory,
O God,
Help us to prioritize the good gifts
Of creativity,
Adventure,
Imagination,
And expression.

As we play with our children,
Be present with us, O God.
As we make memories and forge bonds
With our sons and daughters,
Who won't be young forever,
We thank You for the deep joy
Of replacing grown-up schedules
With the simple magic of
Childhood.

2 Corinthians 5:17; Ephesians 2:10

A Prayer for Walking Together

Christ with us, Christ within us.
Through Your mercy and grace,
Forge a bond as we journey together,
Parent and child,
On hushed country roads
And bustling city streets.
As we hit the pavement
And feel the gravel beneath us,
Help us be slow to speak,
Lingering in the sacred silence
    of together,
And quick to listen
To what is said and left unsaid.

Christ with us, Christ within us.
Give us the wisdom to know
When to hold our children's hands
And when to let them go.
May our children stay rooted in love,
Even as they move forward in freedom.
Give us the courage to climb together
And know when to step back
And cheer our children on
As they embark on their own adventures.

Christ with us, Christ within us.
May our children know You
In the sun on their faces
And the wind at their backs.
Bless this sacred moment

Of time together.
Let us not dwell on the past
Or get lost in the future
But be fully awake
To Your presence
In the present reality of right now.

Christ with us, Christ within us.
In their comings and goings,
In their youth and in their old age,
Give our sons and daughters
Strength for the journey
And rest for when they're weary.
And when they walk,
May they walk paths of peace,
Stopping at the side of the road
For the good of a fellow sojourner.
Thank You for the honor of raising
    children,
And forgive us for the ways we have
    stumbled
In our parenting journeys.

Christ with us, Christ within us.
Thank You for walking alongside us
As we traverse the hills and valleys,
Tending to growing hearts
And souls and bodies and minds.
We pray all this in Your name,
In Christ alone,
Amen.

Ephesians 3:17-19; Irish Blessing; Prayer of Saint Patrick

Give us the
wisdom to know
when to hold our
children's hands
and when to
let them go.

A Prayer for Reading Together

Author of all things bright and beautiful,
We see You in every bedtime story
And every well-worn binding.
We see You in the coffee-stained page
And in the dancing words that come alive.

We see You in the rips and tears and
    folded corners
And in the tales we memorized long ago
When we were children once.
We see You in the books that make our
    babies laugh
And in the books that teach our toothless
    wonders to read
And in the books that bring our growing
    teens into bigger worlds.

We see You in the mysteries and
    adventures.
We see You in the scary stories and the
    sweet ones too.
And we thank You for the magic of
    getting lost in a book,
For we know that in the journey, You're
    hidden in the margins.
We thank You, too, for libraries and
    teachers
And every soul who has ever read a book
    to a child.

We thank You for the imagination to see
    in a new way.
We thank You for inviting us into Your
    story,
The greatest story of all.

John 1:1; Psalm 119:105

PART THREE

Prayers for Times of Transition

MY YOUNGEST CHILD, Abram, recently transitioned from his toddler bed to what he proudly calls his "big-boy bed." As my husband lugged the tiny bed frame down the stairs, I stood in my son's empty room, eyeing the unearthed dust bunnies. I felt something wet on my face. Tears? Were those *tears*? I wiped my cheek and swept the space for the new bed.

I saw Abram as a fresh newborn in the bassinet, a chubby baby in the crib, a potty-training toddler in the tiny hand-me-down bed. How could all these transitions happen so fast? My long-limbed preschooler tugged on my shirt.

"I'm a little sad, Mommy," he whispered as his dad began to build his new twin-size loft bed. "I'm a little scared of the big bed."

I squeezed his hand.

We need a hand to hold when change happens. For me, it's when my babies aren't babies anymore. Maybe for you, it's when your child starts school. Or moves away to college. Maybe it's when the little one you used to play blocks with is suddenly getting married. Or when the daughter who once played with Matchbox cars has passed driver's ed and is now behind the wheel. Time passes. Children get older. It's marvelous and heartbreaking all at once. New experiences and adventures, heartaches and victories loom on the horizon for all of us—and our sons and daughters—but often we can't see what will happen next. We just have to trust (see Proverbs 3:5-6).

So we whisper thanks for what has been and pray for God's provision in what will be.

With Abram's bigger bed came the need for a larger blanket. I headed to the linen closet and pulled out a worn quilt—the one with the seafoam-green stripes that I bought with my own money before I left for college. I tucked it in the four rails of my son's new loft bed and flashed back to the memory of doing the same thing years ago in my college dorm.

We all have different orientations to time. Some of us find ourselves connected to the past, others are rooted in the present, and still others focus on the future. Watching my children transition through ages and stages has somehow swirled my understanding of time. When I made Abram's bed, I flashed forward to him flying the nest. And yet I was also transported back in time, seeing my own history with new eyes. In all my planning and packing for college, I never wondered how my parents might have felt sending their daughter off to college and later watching her enter into marriage. Now I wonder what they prayed as I embarked on new adventures and entered new seasons.

Prayer is a hand to hold, a rooted response to transitional moments in our lives. When we pray, the Holy Spirit intercedes and we're able to loosen our grip and unfurl our grasp on what we want to control, opening ourselves to a posture of listening to and being transformed by what God has done, is doing, and will do.

When Jesus ascended into heaven, His followers found themselves in a time of transition. They had no idea what was happening. Jesus had conquered death, and yet after forty days, He left them again. What would happen next? These devoted believers turned their wonderings into prayer. Men and women gathered in the upper room, marking this passage of sacred, mysterious time together before God.

These prayers were answered with what we call Pentecost. Without warning, a rushing wind filled the whole building. Then, like a wildfire, the Holy Spirit spread among them—the same timeless Spirit who works in us and through us today in our families' own changing seasons (see Acts 1–2).

We don't understand the mystery of God, who existed before time began (see 2 Timothy 1:9) and loved before the foundation of the world (see John 17:24). But in times of transition, prayer anchors us to the hope we have. The liturgies in this collection mark the sacred slivers of time when one season of life ends and another begins. We celebrate the firsts while holding space for the lasts, too. We ask God for courage to let go in this gradual undoing of parenthood, resting in the truth and strengthened in the grace that Jesus Christ is the same yesterday, today, and forever (see Hebrews 13:8).

In this section, you'll find prayers for everything from the first day of school to the celebration of a graduation. You'll find prayers for moving and prayers for when an adult child gets married.

With every time of transition, may we cling to this truth: God has made everything beautiful in its time (see Ecclesiastes 3:11).

A Prayer for Moving

O God of beginnings and endings,
Would You guide us as we prepare to
     move?

You have been with us in the walls of
     this home,
And You will be with us as we go out.

Thank You for the ways these walls have
     held us
And the ways You've hemmed us in with
     Your love.

Every floorboard has a story;
Every room tells a tale.
Help our children to accept this move,
Whether they understand the whys or not.
And let us linger in what was
So that we may look to
What lies ahead.

God, as we pack boxes
And wrap all the fragile pieces,
Layer by layer,
We're reminded of our fragile state,
How easily hearts can break.

May we remember that what makes
     a home
Is who we share it with.
And we thank You for the ways

We have grown together
As we have made this place our home.

May our children reflect on this space
As a place where they were nurtured,
Valued, and loved.
And we ask that You would help us
Unpack these memories
At the next place You have for us.
Spirit, go before us.
Spirit, dwell within us.

We pray for the next mothers and fathers,
Daughters and sons
Who will inhabit this space,
And we pray for the unfathomable
     number
Of parents and children
Who have no place to rest their heads
     tonight.

Even in this time of transition,
May we grow in empathy
To see where and how we can
Better love those among us.

We pray for the neighbors
We will wave goodbye to
And for those who will move in next.

We thank You for the good times
We have had here
And the difficult memories
Shared here too.

As we prepare to leave,
We look at our material abundance.
May we give freely
So others may have the opportunity to
Create their own homes too.

Bless the memories we made,
And be with us as we begin
a new chapter in our lives together.

May our children feel secure
In these times of change.
May they feel Your presence
Even in the unknowing,
And may we trust You
With their futures
And with ours.

Help us to be a house of hospitality
Wherever we live.
Let us live with warmth and welcome,

And always be open to entertaining a
    stranger,
For in doing so, we may welcome angels
    unawares.
And may we always set another place at
    the table.

O God, You move,
And You move us.
Be with us as we close this chapter
And begin a new one.

————————————
Hebrews 13:2; Genesis 12:1-4

O God, You move,
and You move us.
Be with us as we
close this chapter
and begin a new one.

A Prayer for the First Day of Preschool

We can't believe this day is finally here,
O God, Creator of babies,
Who grow so fast.

We see their still-round cheeks
And their skinned knees
And their too-big backpacks,
And we marvel at the sneaky passing
    of time—
Where has our baby gone?

The days have ticked by, hour by hour,
Changing diapers and teaching them how
    to walk.
Now we ask You to guide their steps,
    O God,
In their light-up sneakers
And legs that have lost their toddler rolls,
Giving way to longer, leaner limbs,
Ready to explore.

May we rejoice at their excitement.
May we not diminish their fears.
And may we instill in them confidence
To walk into their first classroom
Full of new faces
And new adventures.

Bless the teachers who have prepared
    for them.

Give them imagination to guide our
    child,
And give them patience, Lord—
So much patience.
May our child make a friend or two
And be transported to lands of
    make-believe
Via centers and color-coded carpets
That have a little magic in them.
We thank You for sand tables and glitter
    glue,
For story time and blocks galore.
May they explore new toys
And get their hands a little dirty too.

When the day is done, O Lord,
Will You bring them safe into our arms?
Because they're preschoolers now,
But they'll always be our babies.

Psalm 107:1; Matthew 19:14; Proverbs 1:8-9

PRAYER TO PRAY WITH CHILDREN

Dear God,
You are with me
At school,
Just like You are at home.
Help me be brave.
Help me have fun.
Help me remember
[Mommy/Daddy] always comes back.
In Jesus' name,
Amen.

A Prayer for the First Day of School

O God of new beginnings,
As this child begins this new school year,
We are reminded that they are Yours
And Yours alone.

We have filled their backpack,
And we ask You to fill their heart
With the joy of new friends
And their mind
With the wonder of learning new
    things.

You are the God of science
And the God of art,
The God of equations
And the God of song.

Be with them,
This piece of my heart,
As they embark on this new adventure,
Becoming more themselves
And needing me less
Every day.

Give them courage
To extend kindness to teachers,
Fellow students,
And even themselves.
May they stand tall in who they are,
And may they find friends to sit with.

Ignite passions in them
For Your world and everything in it.
Spark creativity and stoke the fires of
    imagination.

Give them a heart to see the hurting
And strength to show love in the hallways.
Give them friends,
But help them not to find their worth
    in others.
Give them concentration
And a holy kind of mischief
That keeps them asking why.

Be with their teachers,
Who give so much of themselves.
May they have eyes to see each student
In their own challenges and victories.

God, we know each body and soul
Has a different way of learning.
Help [child's name] find
What helps them learn best
In the ways You've uniquely wired them.

Thank You for all that awaits,
And thank You for the tug in my heart
As I wave goodbye
And watch them enter the doors,
For those are the heartstrings of love.

May this child feel Your love
As they walk the halls,
And may You keep them safe
And bring them safely home.

May they rise to the challenges set in front
  of them,
And may they never be too busy
To bend down and help someone.

Give them focus
And eyes to see someone who could use
  a friend.
Give them imagination,
And may they know the power that lies
  within
A pencil or a paintbrush.
May they learn how understanding history
Can change the future.
And may they see how numbers can come
  together
To make a difference in our world.

God, as they prepare to start the school year,
I wonder if I have taught them enough,
If I have prepared them for this moment.
I care more about their character
Than their academic success.
For what is successful in the eyes of
  the Lord?

I think, too, of the students
For whom school is a refuge
From the storms of life at home.
May they connect with others who truly
  see them,
Not as underresourced or troubled or
  another statistic
But as Your beloved.

We thank You for the gift of education,
For we know it is a privilege
Not all have access to.
Even in our own city,
We know there are inequities
Baked into the bricks of our schools.

In my child's anxieties,
May they find comfort in Your presence.
In their worries,
May they find peace in Your promises.
In their challenges,
May they find victory in Your power.

May they be curious and compassionate.
May they share their lunch with a friend
  in need
Or risk being late to help a lost new
  student find their way.

O God, we give our own worries
And our parental desire for control
To You.
Thank You for the gift of the first day
  of school
And for all the days to come.
May this child learn and grow,
And may I learn and grow too.
Teach us how to love You
And our neighbor
More every day.
Amen.

_____
Joshua 1:9; Deuteronomy 6:5-9

A Prayer for Homeschool

O Jesus, who asked questions and told
   stories,
Help us teach our children to see the
   power of asking why
And to sit in the wonder of someone
   else's story.

Help us kindle curiosity
When the world whispers there's just
   one way.
Help us spark imagination
When the world prefers the way it has
   always been.
Help us fuel passion
When the world shouts that it's easier
   not to care.

O Jesus, who wept and turned water into
   wine,
Help us teach children to weep with those
   who weep
And dance in the joy of those who rejoice.

Help us model empathy
When the world whispers, "Why bother?"
Help us clothe ourselves with
   compassion
When the world prefers a hard heart.
Help us embody love

When the world says some don't
   deserve it.

O Jesus, who knows the aches of
   humanity,
We ask for Your help in teaching our
   children,
Knowing that if we want kids to be
Curious, imaginative, and passionate,
We must create space for it in our home;
Knowing that if we want kids to be
Empathetic, compassionate, and loving,
We must live it out ourselves.

Help us teach our children,
And help us learn from them too.
In Your name we pray,
Amen.

Romans 12:2; Matthew 5:15-16; Colossians 3:12

A Prayer for a Child Leaving Home

O God, as time passes,
I watch the walls of our home
Swell and expand,
And then get smaller, quieter
With the memories of us.

O God, as time passes,
I feel the corners of my heart
Swell and expand,
And then get larger, louder
With the memories of us.

As this child makes their own way
With moving boxes and packing tape,
Hand-me-down couches,
And brand-new dreams of their own,
Guide their heart,
Protect their spirit,
And help me let them go.

For in long days and short years,
I've seen them grow into more
Of who You've made them to be,
And I've grown more into myself too.
As they walk this unfamiliar path,
I see the adult they've become
And the little one they'll always be
    to me.

As they lift heavy boxes up the stairs,
May they know that with them
They carry years of love,
Poured out from parent to child
And child to parent.

As they rest their head at night
In the new dwelling they call home,
May they know that love carries them—
That You always have
And always will—
Through life's unexpected journeys,
Yesterday's dark nights,
And tomorrow's bright mornings.

As they rise in the light of a new day,
Help their feet find the right path
For where to go and how to walk
    in love
In this big world where
Beauty and brokenness coexist.

Whisper into their hearts
The road to follow as they embark
On this new journey—
One they must navigate on their own.
O God, lead them when we cannot,
For we cannot prepare
The journeys our children must take.
And we pray that somehow,
Through the years,
We have prepared our children
For the journeys set ahead for them.

On the twisting roads
And winding paths,
May they know that they never need
    to knock
And that they'll always have a place
In our heart
And in our home.
_____

Psalm 25:4-5

As they rise in the
light of a new day,
help their feet find
the right path for
where to go and
how to walk in love.

A Prayer for Learning to Drive

O God, we entrust our new driver to You.
How could it be
That Matchbox cars and Power Wheels
Have given way
To driver's ed certificates
And a shiny hunk of metal?

O God, parenting is the gradual undoing,
And we have to let them go
To dream their own dreams
And take on their own adventures.
But in this moment,
It feels like too much
To watch them drive away.

We knew these
Mile markers of independence were
    coming,
And still they're a lot to behold.
For so long, we have tried to keep
Our sons and daughters safe.
We have tried to protect them.
But God, we know our kids
Are really Yours,
And we ask You to watch over them
As their world expands a little more.

Thank You for the privilege
Our children have to learn to drive.

May they steward this honor
And responsibility well.
And Lord, we know that all young drivers
Are not equal on the road.
We lament the ways
Parents of Black and Brown children
Must have different conversations
About how to travel and how to drive.
Be near to all who
Rend their hearts
As they buckle their seat belts.

Bless the road, Lord,
That will bring our children home
To a family that loves them,
To a family that is so proud of them,
To a family that will never tire
Of waiting up
To welcome them
Back into our arms,
Back into our home.

Deuteronomy 31:8

A Prayer for Graduation

O God, Creator of beginnings and
   endings,
We pray for our graduate.
Walk ahead of them and beside them
As they step into a big world
Littered with loss but glittering with hope.

You were there for every
newborn squeal and first step and lost
   tooth.
Remind us that You are with them now,
   too,
As our child looks ahead
And wonders what is to come.

We lament the ways we have confused
productivity with worth
And projected that onto our children.
And we pray that our graduate will know
Their belovedness
Doesn't rest in their accomplishments.

We pray for an emboldened generation
That refuses to accept the systems they've
   inherited.
And we pray that we will support them
As they use their imagination and energy,
Passion and creativity
To love the world You made and the
   people in it.

O God, Creator of beginnings and
   endings,
We pray for our graduate.
Be with us as we celebrate in new ways.
And when we cannot celebrate,
Be with us as we cry.

Give them, and us,
A new lens for seeing the world
And hope for the future
In Jesus Christ, our Lord.

Hebrews 11:1; Colossians 3:17

Walk ahead of
and beside
our child
as they step into
a big world
littered with loss
but glittering
with hope.

A Prayer for Letting Go

O God, in whom all creation exists
And who exists in all creation,
Give us the strength
To loosen our parental grip
And let go
Of what
And of who
Were never truly ours in the first place.

The days felt so long,
And now it's time to step back
So the one
Who will always be so little to us
Can move forward
To take their wobbly first steps
Into adulthood.

In the places we cannot be,
Help us trust You are there
With the mothering spirit of an eagle,
Rousing her chicks and hovering over
    her young,
Spreading her wings to take them up
And carry them to safety.

In the places we cannot be,
Help us know You are there
With the fathering spirit of a shepherd,
Protecting Your lambs and caring for
    the young,

Leaving the ninety-nine to protect the one
And carry that one to safety.

As our child makes their place in the
    world,
Be the fresh air that fills their lungs.
Lead them to places of rest,
And propel them to keep going
When they're road-weary
And not sure if they can go on.
Build hope into their hearts
So they know they're never alone—
Not for one minute, O Lord,
Not even for one moment.

Let every act of parenting's past
And parenting's future
Be an act of love,
O Lord.
Help us remember
That even in this dance
Of stepping back
And letting go,
You'll hold them
As they journey on.
And You'll hold us, too,
As we watch them soar.
And You'll never,
Not once,
Let us down.

Deuteronomy 32:11; Matthew 18:12-14; Psalm 23

A Prayer for a Son or Daughter Who Is Single

We come to You so grateful
To watch our child
Grow into the person
You've created them to be.

We come to You in awe
As we see them embrace life.

We come to You with joy
As we watch their personality emerge
And see the gifts You've given them
Break through to our weary world.

We come to You to give thanks
For exactly who they are,
Right at this very moment.
May they feel the warmth and welcome
Of community inside the church
And inside our family.
May they know that their value and
　　their worth
Does not rest in a relationship status
Amid a culture where relationships
Can often be idols.

We come to You asking for a spirit
　　of listening
For the songs You've placed
In the hearts of our grown child.
Help us not to assume,

To let go of unspoken expectations,
And to honor their journey
As we watch them fly the nest
And make their own way.

We come to You asking for healing
Where yesterday's hurt lingers in their
　　heart.
We ask for hope to fill their every
　　tomorrow.
And we pray that wherever
Their journey with You takes them,
That they will be attentive and receptive
To Your formative work
In their heart and mind,
Body and soul.

We come to You with hearts full
　　of gratitude
As we marvel at the wonder
Of seeing a child
Become their own person,
Reflecting Your light
In their joys and trials.
May they love You, O God,
And love their neighbor.
May they feel love in friendships
And in family relationships too.
May they know they are
Never on this journey
Alone.

Deuteronomy 31:8

A Prayer for the Marriage of a Son or Daughter

O God, we love
Because You first loved us.
And it's that abiding love
That we as parents
Pray we have passed on to our child,
In our strengths and in our failings.
We pray that we have given them
Roots to grow from.

As this new couple journeys together
Toward You, O Lord,
Tend to their hearts.
Help them cultivate
A flourishing life together.
Help them nourish the soil
Of their relationship
So that they may embody
Love, joy, and peace,
Patience, kindness, and goodness,
Faithfulness, gentleness, and self-control.

As they prepare for marriage
And commit to each other,
May they know the gift
Of fully giving
And receiving.
Be with them as they
Enter into this partnership.

Wrap them in Your mercy;
Bind them with Your grace.
Give them strength
To admit their weaknesses.
Give them courage
To be vulnerable.
Give them light to cling to
When the road ahead is dark.
Give them a hand to hold
When thunder rumbles
And lightning cracks.

May their love be an offering
To each other
And to You.
May they bring their whole selves,
Even the broken parts,
To each other.
May they be gentle
As they hold each other's fragile hearts.
May they be tender
As they hold each other's breakable
    spirits.

Strengthen their relationship, O Lord,
As they bring together
The profoundly human
And the deeply sacred.
Give them words to express expectations
And call out beauty in each other.
Give them the gift of communication
And the ability to sit in silence with
    each other
When words won't do.

May their marriage
And commitment to each other
Be patient,
Be gentle,
And be kind.
Bless their commitment
To be coadventurers,
Colaborers,
And cocreators
In life together,
Rooted in You.

Their souls
Will take many shapes
As seasons come.
Be near in the celebrations
And in the quiet doubts too.
May they walk in
Mutual submission to each other
And joint submission to Christ.
As they create their own family,
May they know they do not subtract
From their family of origin
But rather add to our vibrant tapestry
Of life together.

May they commit to being present with
    each other
And to pursuing their own gifts and
    callings too.
May they, together, love their neighbors
With hospitality and warmth.
Bring them encouragers for the journey
    too.

Give them laughter when they're weary.
Give them openness when they don't
    understand.
Give them hope when they're tired.

May the challenging moments
Strengthen their bonds.
May they be a safe space
For the other to land
And heal from hurts.
Give them eyes to see each other
When darkness closes in.
Give them arms to catch each other
When one is too weak.
Give them voices to sing to each other
When one has forgotten the words.

May they be rooted
And established in love:
A love that speaks truth to each other,
A love that lays down weapons,
A love that honors,
A love that hopes,
A love that never fails.

Galatians 5:22-23; 1 Corinthians 13; Ephesians 5:21;
Ephesians 3:17-19

PART FOUR

Prayers for a Weary World

PARENTING IS HUMBLING. As we raise children, we have countless opportunities, from morning to night, to remember our humanity and our need for a God who restores and redeems.

The Christian life doesn't protect us from the sorrows of this present reality; rather, it equips us to enter into suffering as Christ did—and does—for us.

While each of my kids has their own array of tablets and devices, one thing I've felt passionate about is limiting their exposure to live TV. I'm aware of the ways commercials shape young, developing brains, and as a former journalist, I know all too well the vitriol spilled on cable news. But one rainy day, my son begged me to watch a talent competition, and I acquiesced. We collected blankets and sank onto the couch, balancing bowls of popcorn on our knees as we gathered around the glow of the TV.

After marveling at acrobats and giggling at comedians, it was time for a commercial break. Before I could find the remote, a political campaign ad started right in. The video clips looked like a depiction of hell—images of fire, crying babies, and blaring ambulances, with a disembodied voice warning that this was what would happen if the opposing candidate was elected. My kids looked at me, wide eyed, and before I could change the channel, the ad was over and we were being told by a woman standing in a kitchen that there was truly only one good type of paper towel.

My husband and I exchanged glances. At that moment I knew I could ignore what my kids had just witnessed or I could enter into a conversation—a difficult one—that I wasn't sure I had the words for. I said a quick prayer under my breath (sometimes "God, help me!" is the best I can muster), and gathered my crew around, inviting them to share about what we had just seen.

We talked about our country's broken political system and how sometimes people—even grown-ups, even leaders—lie or say things to scare others. We talked about being wise consumers of media, and we found ourselves lamenting our world, but also learning from the experience together. How does what we know to be true about our merciful, just, righteous God tell us about how we understand the world?

We don't need all the answers; we just need to be present.

As parents, we don't have to be experts. We're not called to be theological geniuses or top scholars. Instead, we are to guide our children and whisper into their hearts the most excellent love story of all. Jesus didn't avoid corrupt systems, tough topics, or aching hearts. He specifically entered into our pain and suffering—our collective brokenness and our individual sorrows. Even in His divinity, Jesus wept at the loss of His friend Lazarus (see John 11:33-35). And we, too, weep with our children. We hold their hearts with the same care that God holds ours. We weep with those who weep (see Romans 12:15). We do not avoid our preschooler's sobs as they grieve the death of their goldfish, just as we don't avoid sitting in the reality of raising children in unjust systems and inequitable economic structures.

I often underestimate the vastness of God. When I stand at the edge of the ocean or when I learn about the complexities of the galaxies, I'm reminded of my smallness—and what a comfort that is. We don't need all the answers, but as we pray, we're reminded that we have the Holy Spirit and access to a well of infinite love that won't run dry.

We enter into lament with prayers of holy heartache (see 2 Corinthians 1:5).

As we witness the weary world around us, we acknowledge the ways we have fallen short of the glory of God (see Romans 3:23), and we ask for reconciliation, reparation, and renewal. What a profound gift it is to guide our children in these conversations. Perhaps you came from a family or church that avoided pain—communal or personal. But it's never too late to allow the Spirit to crack open our hearts so that we may enter into our children's suffering, just as Christ comes into ours (see John 14:26). Christ ushered in a new reality—a Kingdom of God that is now and not yet.

While we ache for the day every tear will be wiped away, we are invited onto a new path of walking together toward God's beckoning arms. We no longer have to avoid the broken realities of our outer and inner worlds, because Scripture shows us a new way. In the Psalms, we see David's prayers of lament stamped throughout. David grieved. He knew God's goodness and clung to that truth, even amid his pain.

We don't have to have all the answers to the pain our families may face. But we have been called to enter into one another's suffering—to bear one another's burdens (see Galatians 6:2). Our children are watching. Every day, their perceptive hearts sense that things are not as they should be. As parents, we have the sacred gift and responsibility of guiding them as they learn about themselves, the world, and the God who made everything—and is making all things new.

From grieving the death of a loved one to talking with our children about racism, these prayers of lament help us begin to put words to the groans of creation (see Romans 8:19-23).

As generations have prayed before us, *Lord, have mercy. Christ, have mercy.*

A Prayer for Infertility

O God who sees
All that we cannot see,
We come to You
With the ache and yearning
To be a parent.

Lord, we have prayed,
And we wonder if You hear us
Calling out to You.
For still, the nursery is empty,
And our hearts feel poured out
And left forgotten.

We walk this road
Littered with tests
And doctor's appointments
And dashed dreams,
And we wonder if You are
Truly with us in the waiting.

As we've taken paths
We never thought we'd walk,
We pray for permission for our weary
    bodies
And souls
To rest
When we're not sure we can take another
    detour.

O God, You have not forgotten us.
Help us know that our unmet hopes
Have not been divine punishments,
And remind us
Again and again and again
You are with us in the unknown.

Help us trust Your ways,
Even when Your ways
Look different from ours.
Help us as we discern next steps.
Guide us when we're not sure where to go.
Lead us when it feels like
Our compass is spinning in all directions.

Carry us through disappointments.
Give us community that loves and
    supports.
Help us lean into those who love us;
Help us trust that You are there.

We pray that Your mercies
Really would be new each morning
And that we would have strength to face
    each new day.
You know the ache of our hearts,
And You are not blind to the emotions
    we feel.
As we receive yet another baby shower
    invitation
Or see another announcement online,
Give us grace to love through the pain,
And grant us rest when we need to protect
    our hearts.

Give us words to put to our hurt.
Give us loved ones who will hear them,
Receiving pieces of our hearts and holding
    them with care,
With no rush to put a bow on our pain,
For infertility has felt like anything
    but a gift.

Help us see Your goodness around us.
Whisper hope into the corners of our
    hearts,
The tucked-away spaces
No one else ever sees.

You are the God who sees,
And we ask that You would make a way
For our family to grow.
Help us to believe that You are still good
And You are still with us
On this unexpected journey.

You call us Your children,
Your beloved daughters and sons.
Help us stand in that identity
No matter what.

———————

Psalm 130:5; 1 John 3:1

A Prayer for Pregnancy Loss

O Lord, our hearts are broken
At the loss of this life
And what could have been.

Let our tears be a prayer
As we cry out to You.
We don't understand the loss of this
    pregnancy,
And we're not sure we ever will.

O Jesus, You wept,
And we pray that You will wipe every tear.
Will You be with us
As we sit in silence
When the tears have run dry?

Lord, You are not afraid of our emotions,
And we give each one of ours to You.
Will You help us name what we're feeling?

Will You comfort us when we feel alone?
Will You protect us from feelings of guilt
    or shame as we grieve?
O Helper, Comforter, Protector,
We come to You.

As we mourn, help us not lose hope.
As we grieve, help us hold tight to Your
    promises.
And when the time comes,
Will You help us heal?
Will You mend our hearts
And grow in us a sense of light in the
    darkness?

Lord, we ask for Your Spirit
To wrap us in a warm embrace.
Hold us tight in Your love,
And let us cling to Your goodness,
For You have not forgotten us,
And we are not alone.

Thank You for letting us come to You
With our tear-rimmed eyes and dripping
    noses,
With our shouting and our silent sorrow.

Will You ignite in us a spark
That one day our hearts
May be a place to kindle hope
And even joy again?

We pray all things in Your name,
Amen.

Psalm 34:18; Psalm 56:8

As we mourn, help us not lose hope. As we grieve, help us hold tight to Your promises.

A Prayer for the Death of a Child

Our Father in heaven,
This is a prayer
No one should ever have to pray.
How do we find the words
As we grieve the death
Of our baby?
Lord, hear our prayer.

We are tired.
We are raw.
We are bone weary and exhausted.
We are angry and confused.
Lord, hear our prayer.

We ache for the ways our family
And our hearts
Will never be the same.
And we cry out to You as we mourn
The light the world has lost.
Lord, hear our prayer.

Will You sit with us?
As we sit in deafening silence,
As we sit in our shouting cries,
As we sit in our hurricane of emotions,
And as we sit in the scariest space
Of feeling nothing at all,
Lord, hear our prayer.

Will You be with us?
In our questions,
In our fears,
We ask You to meet us,
To hold us when we can't stand,
To remind us that You'll never leave us.
Lord, hear our prayer.

We want to trust You in the unknown.
We want to believe You'll hold our
    child
Now that our arms are empty.
We admit that we don't know how,
So we ask for Your help
And Your comfort
And Your hope
And Your blessed assurance
That we will someday see our child
    again—
And what a great rejoicing that will be.
Lord, hear our prayer.

We thank You for the precious time we
    had together,
Though it was much too short
And we may always wonder what could
    have been.
We thank You for the moments
Shared between us
And ask that we will never
Lose sight of those memories
We clutch close to our chests.
Lord, hear our prayer.

We pray for those who love us
But cannot understand our grief.
Sometimes their words,
In a rush to be hopeful,
Hurt our hearts.
And sometimes their silence,
In their fear of not knowing what to say,
Leaves us wounded.
Lord, hear our prayer.

O God who knows every ache
Of what it is to have a child die,
We believe;
Help us in our unbelief.
Help us cling to You, Jesus.
You are making all things new.
You will make beauty from these ashes.
You will restore our souls.
You are a God that keeps promises,
Who will never leave or forsake,
And we cling to that as we grieve.
Lord, hear our prayer.

We don't know how to hold it all,
So will You hold us, O Lord,
When we feel like we would give anything
To hold our child one more time?
We ask You to be near
As we walk this long journey
Of grief and of healing.
Lord, hear our prayer.

Romans 8:38-39; Psalm 34:18; John 10:27-29;
Psalm 147:3; Mark 9:24

A Prayer for the NICU

O God, creator and sustainer of life,
We come to You
With all our worries and what-ifs
And pray for this precious life
You have brought into the world.

We thank You for the gift of modern
    medicine,
Of skilled doctors and nurses
Who heal the smallest among us.
And yet, too, we grieve
For the steps forward and then back,
For the tubes and machines,
For the sterile rooms and fluorescent
    lights,
For the hospital coffee and bloodshot
    eyes,
For the dreams put on hold
Or changed entirely.

Lord, help us remember
That You love our baby,
Still fresh from the womb,
More than we could ever imagine.
For if the love we feel for them
Is so strong it overflows,
We know Your perfect love
Is big enough to hold together

This tiny life so new to us
But so known to You.

We wish we could take their suffering
And make it our own.
Every poke, prick, and prod—
We would bear it all
If it meant they would be okay.
We know this kind of love
Comes from You, Jesus—
A God who bled out in love.

We pray for Your presence
In these hospital walls
And for the times we are apart.
We pray for patience
When healing takes time,
Ounce by ounce.
We pray for bonds to form
And scars to heal.

We are scared but know You are strong.
We are sad but know You are
    compassionate.
We are worried but know You are good.

Give us imagination to picture life together
Without scrubbing in.
We pray for healing
And for hope to hold on to.

Help us trust You.
Help this newborn grow.

Help us advocate.
Help this newborn heal.
Help us rest.
Help this newborn rest.

We lay all this at Your feet
And ask You now to give us hope.
For we are weary,
But You are good.

_____

Psalm 71:6; Psalm 27:14

A Prayer for Postpartum Depression

Lord, bless the mother
Who is fighting postpartum depression,
Having a hard time catching her breath,
Wondering if You're really near.

Lord, bless the mother
Who is tired and afraid.
Be near in the dark nights
And the already-exhausted mornings.

Lord, bless the mother
Who does not feel like herself
As she goes through the motions,
Seeing herself in a fog.

Lord, bless the mother
Who wonders what's wrong,
Rocking her baby,
Not recognizing herself.

Lord, bless the mother
Who feels completely alone.
Give her community
To tangibly care for her.

Lord, bless the mother
Who seeks healing under the medical care
Of a doctor or therapist.
Prevent any shame or guilt from clouding
      her heart.

Lord, bless the mother
Who thinks her mental health is her fault.
Protect her from lies,
And give healing and hope to her body
      and soul.

2 Corinthians 12:9; Romans 5:1-5

A Prayer Before a Child's Hospitalization

Help me remember, O Lord,
That nothing surprises You
And no need is too great
For Your mighty hand.

O Lord, I ache to fix things,
To heal my child,
To protect them from suffering.
And though I wish I were in control,
I'm fighting to trust that You alone
   are God.

As they prepare to don a gown
And be whisked away from my hands,
Go where I cannot, O God.
Fill the doctors and nurses
With compassion, confidence, and care
As they help my child toward healing.

Spirit, hover over every poke and prick,
Every doctor's decision,
And every piece of medical equipment.
Thank You for the gift of modern medicine
And every skilled professional.
Steady the hands
That hold my child.
O God, as I pray for my child,
I pray, too, for the mothers and fathers
Who ache for their children to receive
   this level of care

But are unable to because of where
   they live.

Help my child to be courageous
In the face of the unknown.
Help me be a soothing presence
As we say goodbye
And as I trust You to bring us back
   together soon.

Spirit, be with [child's name].
Be near, O Lord.
Heal their body and spirit,
And be with me
As I sit on a plastic waiting room chair,
Watching the clock
As I wait with bated breath.

I pray for healing to come.
Help me trust those caring for my child.
Help me remember their oath
To do no harm.
Help me remember
You have given us every reason to trust You,
O Lord.

You are good, O Lord.
You love [child's name]
More than I do—a truth almost
   unfathomable.
I cling to Your truth like a life preserver,
Holding me afloat on a sea of unknown.
Give me peace
As I turn every anxiety over to You.

Psalm 28:7; Isaiah 41:10

70

A Prayer for When Your Child Receives a Diagnosis

O Lord, You love our child infinitely
     more
Than we can wrap our minds around.
Help us remember that truth
When we arise and when we go to sleep
     at night.
For with this new diagnosis,
Our heads are spinning
And our hearts are aching.

O Lord, may every act of love be a prayer
     to You—
Every visit to a specialist,
Every late night spent researching,
Every parking spot in the hospital garage.

You hold our child in the palm of
     Your hand,
And we thank You that You have
     entrusted
The great joys and sorrows of this
     parenting journey to us.

O Lord, we pray for our child—
For comfort and for unexpected strength,
For rest and for rivers of peace,
For joy and for abundant laughter,
For doctors and for science

To converge with the peace
That surpasses all understanding.

We love from a deep well,
And yet sometimes our bones are dry
And we wonder why.
Why our child? Why us? Why this?

Help us know we are not alone
In these heavy questions.
Help us know that we can turn to You
With every wondering of the soul.

Give us eyes to see the beauty
In the beating heart in front of us,
And give us the gift of vulnerability
As we offer the broken parts of our hearts
     to You.
Wrap Your arms around our child.
Help us to remember that You have loved
     them
With a great love,
And while we are invited into their story,
We do not have to have all the answers.
We are simply called to show up,
For You alone are God.
And we are allowed to remove the weight
Of parenting perfection
From our shoulders.

In the laughter and in the tears,
And in the steps forward
And in the steps back,
May we keep our hearts centered
On the great truth that

You will never leave us or forsake us.
And may we live in the promise that
It is really true.

This may be a journey that
Takes us on unexpected paths,
But You will never leave Your flock.
Thank You for always pursuing us,
Even when we have felt the most alone.

We pray for wholeness and healing
In whatever form that takes right now,
And for perseverance and peace
In the promises of Your mighty love.

2 Corinthians 1:3-4; 1 Peter 5:7

We pray for wholeness
and healing in whatever
form that takes right now,
and for perseverance and
peace in the promises
of Your mighty love.

A Prayer for a Child with a Disability

O God, You are an artist.
Your glory is in every swirl
And imprint of our lives.

You know our child intimately—
Their very nature reflects Your glory.
You have knit them together in the womb,
And not a sliver of DNA
Or one strand of hair
Goes unnoticed or unloved
By You.

We pray for our child,
That we would be able to meet
Their complex needs.
And when we cannot meet them, O Lord,
Give us the right people at the right time
To enter into life with us.
Give us community to surround
Our child with understanding and
    compassion,
Expertise and empathy,
Hope and love.

Help our child to know they are not
    alone
In their personal challenges and victories.
Surround them with love all the days
    of their lives.

Be with us on the dark nights
When we are awake,
Worried about what the future will
    look like
For our child,
For our family,
And for us.

Give us eyes to see beyond this world,
For our children have much to show us.

Help us not diminish our child
By defining them by a diagnosis,
But let us celebrate our child
For exactly who they are.
In the doctor's appointments and waiting
    rooms,
Give us peace.
In the research and the therapies,
Give us hope.
In the classrooms and the medical trials,
Give us strength.

Help us to avoid trap of comparison,
And lead us to see that our lives
Are not marked by what we do
But rather by who we are
And who we love.

Help us to shout the worth of the child
You have placed in our lives.
And when our voices grow hoarse,
Help us to know when to rest.

Empower our child to know
They are valued and worthy.
Give us new mercies each morning
As we rise to do the often-unseen acts
    of love
As we care for our child.

You have created our brains and bodies
In amazing ways.
Help us dance in the broad spectrums
Of Your great love.

Lord, sometimes our great mysteries
Are misunderstood,
And more often than not,
We feel the great chasm between
What is seen and what is unseen.

Will You give us community?
Will You provide respite
When the days are long?
Will You provide bread for the journey
As the years are long?

We thank You for our child's heart,
For in the unique ways they love the
    world,
We feel You more fully.
We thank You for their soul,
For in the ways they are in the world,
We feel You more fully.
We thank You for their body,
For in the ways they experience the world,
We feel You more fully.

We thank You for their brain,
For in the ways they understand the
    world,
We feel You more fully.
Help our family to take each day as it
    comes.
Help us to do the best we can
To come to You in the celebrations and
    struggles.

Transform our hearts, souls, bodies,
    and minds
To be tuned to Your time—
The *kairos* time that gives us perspective,
Not the *chronos* timelines
Of developmental charts and educational
    goals.

In our child's victories and in their
    struggles,
May we be a safe place to land.
In their wins and in their defeats,
May we parent with our arms wide open.
And may we always sense Your presence
    in it all.

Help us to understand more fully the
    mysteries
Of who our child is.
Help us to understand their joys and
    sorrows.
Help us, Lord.
Our child is Yours,
And Your Spirit is among us.

Help us to neither define our child
Solely by their disability
Nor shy away from exactly who they are.
Thank You for making our child,
For they truly are beautiful and wonderful
And made by You.
————————————
Psalm 139:13-16; Romans 15:13; Lamentations 3:22-23

A Prayer for Divorce

O God, we come to You
Reminded that You are
Present in every transition
And in every ounce of tension.
We ask You to make Your presence known
In the pushes and pulls
Of divorce.

Our life together has changed, O Lord,
But You remain constant
As we hold an array of emotions
And walk with our children
Toward healing and wholeness.
We hold space for what has been lost
And space for the hope we may someday
    gain, too.

Lord, we pray for community
To surround our family
With care and compassion.
And we pray that we will extend that grace
To ourselves, too.

Be with us in the awkward spaces
We never imagined we'd find ourselves in,
    Lord.
Help us know You are ever-present
In every court date and custody
    agreement,

In the deep stretches of loneliness
And in the glimmers of hope, too,
That one day things might get better.

We come to You and ask for Your help
To walk toward forgiveness
For those who have hurt us.
And if we have inflicted pain,
We ask for Your forgiveness,
For we know that You are forgiving,
Abounding in love for those who call
    to You.

This is a plot twist, Lord,
And we have knots in our stomachs.
For there are days when our hearts are
    tattered
And we cry out to You, asking why.
Help us remember
This story isn't over.
You are a God who shows up
And keeps showing up,
Even when we feel like
We have nothing left to give.
Help us remember
Nothing comes as a surprise to You.

In the misunderstandings,
You understand us.
In the fractured expectations,
You breathe new life.

Lord, be near in the big emotions
And the no-easy-answers.

We pray our kids will know they're loved.
May they hold no shame or guilt
Over the dissolution of this marriage,
And may they know a parent's love
    doesn't stop
Even if partnerships sometimes do.

Help us navigate relationships
That have changed.
Help us rebuild new normals
And see You in new ways.

God, You are not finished with us,
With the story of our family.
We need You, Lord,
In the messy middle,
In the unexpected endings,
And in the new beginnings.

Psalm 46:1-2; Hebrews 10:23

A Prayer for Job Loss

O God who provides for each day,
Help us trust You.
Help us be humble enough to
Accept help when we need a listening ear
Or a helping hand
Or the simple compassion of another.
And help us to be brave enough
To keep trusting
That You love us in our vulnerabilities
And You will provide for us in our need.

O God, we just want to provide for
    our kids,
To give them a family they can rely on,
A home with warm beds,
Full cupboards,
And room to be themselves.
But right now, we aren't sure how
We'll even pay the bills.
We want to give our kids
What they need
And sometimes even
What they want.

We know money doesn't buy life,
But sometimes it provides comfort.
And now with this job loss,
We're not sure what to do.
Where will we go from here?

What will we do? Who will we be?
Give us new hope to begin again.
Set us on a new journey
Full of hope over bitterness,
Imagination over cynicism.

God, help us know that our worth
Is more than a paycheck.
Help us trust You
With our family's future
That was never ours to hold anyway.
The road ahead is filled with unknowns,
But we know You are good
And You love us.
May that be enough.

Psalm 130:5; John 16:33

A Prayer for the Death of a Loved One

God, our creator of life
And sustainer of breath
In our own lungs
And in the lungs of our children,
Give us words to say
At the loss of life.
And when we have lost our words,
Give us the gift of presence,
Of sitting in the dark
With an arm around a small shoulder,
Pulling them in
And holding them close.

Give us answers
When we need them,
And may we have the strength
To say "I don't know"
When we don't know.

May we remember
That death
Is a part of life
And life
Is a part of death.

May You comfort
The hearts and souls
Of our children

Who wonder
And worry.

May You soothe
Anxieties
And remind us that
Tears are good
And welcome, even—
Reminders that
We feel,
We care,
And we are.

We pray as Jesus prayed:
"On earth as it is in heaven."
And we find hope
That one day
Every tear will be wiped away.

Help us remember that
Our children are not alone
In this universe.
Guide us
As we enter into painful conversations
With empathy,
Compassion,
And care.

We pray this to the author
And finisher
Of our faith,
In Jesus Christ our Lord,
Amen.

_____

Matthew 6:10; Revelation 21:4-5; John 14:1-3; Hebrews 12:2

A Prayer for the Death of a Pet

O God who sees
And holds our tears,
We give You our sadness
As we grieve the loss
Of our beloved companion.

We miss their presence
And how they knew
Just how to make us
Feel loved,
Just how to remind us
Of the love that connects us all.

We pray for our kids,
Who are hurting
As they try to understand
Life and death
And where You are in it all.

May we hold space for the big questions
That our little ones may have.
Give us answers and grant us grace
To know when to sit with them in the
    quiet.
And may we be a soft place
For their tears and their wonderings
To land.

We are sad, O God.
We wish we had one more day together.

We miss our pet's presence
And the way they nestled into our hearts
Just so.

Guide us as our children
Look to us for notes on how to grieve,
And may we allow them to process
On their own timelines and in their
    own ways.

For the memories, we give thanks.
For the void our pet has left in our hearts,
We give thanks too.
Thank You for the memories made
    together,
For the ways pets become
Beloved members of our family,
And the way they'll always be
Beloved parts of our family's heart.

Philippians 4:6-7; Matthew 11:28-30

May we be
a soft place
for our children's
tears and their
wonderings
to land.

A Prayer After a Natural Disaster

You are a God of power,
And through Jesus,
You chose to show us Your strength
Through Your gentle love.

When the winds blow and the earth
    quakes,
When foundations crumble and oceans
    rise,
We look to You as we pick up the pieces.

We're reminded of our smallness
And the reality that our world
Is not as it should be.

We are shaken by what has happened—
The destruction, the damage, the disarray.
And for all the loss, Lord,
We grieve and give our tears to You.

Lord, we're looking for rainbows,
But sometimes they're hard to see.
Help us provide comfort and care to our
    children.
Help us take shelter in the comfort of
    Your wings.
And ignite a light of hope inside of us
As we assess the damage
And band together to rebuild.

In our loss, may we grow in empathy
For the devastation of our neighbors.
And may we grow, too, in compassion
For our global neighbor,
For whom tragedy and devastation are
    never far,
Even for children.

May our hearts and also our actions
Be shored up in love.
If we have two, may we give one.
And if we have one,
May we be ready to share.

We pray for those whose homes have been
    destroyed.
May Your people be a beacon of hope
In the darkness
For those whose hopes have been
    demolished.

We know these are not acts of Your
    punishment
But groans of creation.
And even in the loss, You are here,
Guiding us.

Help us help others.
May we point to helpers as our children
Are scared or confused.
And may we always be willing to help
Someone who needs a hand.
May we model this to our children,
Who are always watching.

For those who weep,
May we weep with them.
For those who ask why,
May we sit in the silence of the unknown.
Lord, You are our lighthouse.

Our comforter, our shepherd,
May we, our children, and our neighbors
Remember Your love,
Even as—maybe especially as—
we sit in the unknown.

In the warnings to take cover,
In the sirens and news alerts,
In the earth's trembling,
We think of those with no home to
    board up
Or no family to check in with.
And we give thanks
For the first responders and power-line
    workers,
For shelter and communities coming
    together,
For rebuilding stronger than before,
For a firm foundation in You.

---

2 Corinthians 4:8-9; Genesis 9:15-16; Romans 12:15;
1 Timothy 6:19

A Prayer for Gun Violence in School

O God of protection and peace,
We come to You weary,
Heartbroken, and afraid.

How do we explain to our child
What it means to practice an active
    shooter drill at school
When we ourselves don't have the words?
When we ourselves barely understand?

How has it gotten this dangerous
To be a child
In a desk
In a classroom?

We grieve for innocence lost by way
    of violence.
Lord, hear our prayer.

We ache for teachers who must prepare
    for the unthinkable.
Lord, hear our prayer.

We pray for every mother and father
Who is forever changed by the
    unimaginable—
The death of a child
At the hands of gun violence.

We rub our eyes and will our minds to
    stop the imagery,
For it is too much to hold.
And yet, some must hold it.

O Lord who said let the little children
    come to Me,
We have sent our teachers to first-aid
    seminars
But have not cried out to You to stop
    the bleeding.

Give us the imagination to see a world
Without violence.
Give us a Kingdom imagination to create
    a better future
For our children and their children.

We are scared, Lord.
We even wonder how You can allow
Mass shootings of children to happen.

When we walk our children to their
    classrooms,
We lament that we quietly assess
How close their tiny cubbies are to the
    front door.

But we know this is not Your way,
    O Lord.
Help us beat our swords into plowshares.
Help us put down our swords,
Collectively and individually.

Speak peace into our children's hearts
As their little minds try to comprehend
The possibilities of what they're
        practicing for.

Our job as parents is to keep our children
        safe—
How do we do so?
Give us eyes to see.
Give us new vocabularies
And courageous hearts to champion
Our children.

Lord, heal our collective wounds.
Lord, heal our individual hearts.
That crack into pieces
Every time our kids step onto the school
        bus.

Lord, may we see into Your upside-down
        Kingdom.

Give us courage and boldness
To plead the case of our children.
Deliver us from the evil one,
And may our action for a more peaceable
        world
For our children
Be a prayer of its own.
Lord, hear our prayer.

_____

Mark 10:13-16; Micah 4:3; John 14:27; Romans 12:21; Matthew 5:9

A Prayer for Talking about Racism with Children

O compassionate and merciful Christ,
Help us remember even our youngest
Are perceptive to our world.
Guide us to validate their feelings
And meet our children where they are.

Help us talk about racism with our
    children,
O Word that became flesh,
And as we teach them about racism,
Naming it for what it is,
Keep us from minimizing racism's
    legacy.
Help us commit to educating early
    and often.

O holy, mysterious Spirit,
Help us make space for
Big questions from little hearts,
Even if we can't answer them.
Help us sit in the tension
And resist the urge to flee the
    uncomfortable,
For we know many do not have that
    privilege.

O Author of our faith,
Make our speech clear and honest.

Give us specific and direct language;
Root our words in history and truth.
And for the future, Lord, give us hope.

O Comforter who weeps,
Help us sit in a spirit of peace
As we wade into conversations,
But help us not resist our own deep
    emotions.
Help us embrace our humanity and,
    in turn,
Show our children
That it's right and righteous
For all of us to be upset about injustice,
That it's right and holy and of You
To make marginalized voices heard.
Help us repent of and lament
Any harm we may have caused,
And heal us from the ways
We may have benefited from,
Or been hurt by,
Oppressive systems that are not of You.

O good Shepherd who cares,
Help us make space for our children's
    curiosity
About the world and all its people.
These conversations may be difficult,
But we know they are necessary.
Help us listen to Your promptings,
    O God,
As we support our children
In standing for Your boundless love
For all humankind.

O reconciling Christ,
Who calls us to be peacemakers,
We pray for true unity rooted in
    Your justice.
And in all things,
Help our families turn
From the worn-out ways of the world
To the life-giving ways of Your Kingdom,
Now and forevermore.
Amen.

———————————
Matthew 7:12; 1 John 4:19-21; 2 Corinthians 5:18; Colossians 1:20

O holy, mysterious
Spirit, help us make
space for big questions
from little hearts,
even if we can't
answer them.

A Prayer for When Your Child Sees Something Scary on the News

O God, You hold the world in
    Your hands,
So You know when we hurt
And when we ache.
You feel it too—
The beat of
Our heaving hearts,
Reverberating into You.

Our children are perceptive,
And their brains and hearts
Have absorbed news of
Unspeakable things.
How do we see You in these headlines?
How do we pray when we don't have
    words?

Help us enter into conversations
with our child.
Let Your love be a raft
When we feel like we're sinking.
Help us resist the urge to say
Situations are better than they are.
Help us to be honest
And gentle
As we invite our child to express their
    emotions—

Their sadness, their fear, their frustration.
For in naming our feelings,
We can move through them together.

As we sit with our child
And stare into the brokenness of
    humanity,
We pray for eyes to see You.
May we learn from our child
What it is to be moved to tears.
And will You give our family
Hearts that cling to hope
Even when life is scary
Or feels out of control?

O God, You are constant
In turbulent times.
You are unchanging,
And we can trust You
To be with us
Even when we feel
Like we're reaching out for You
    in the dark.

God, give us wisdom to know
How to parent our child
As they metabolize the pain of our world.
Help us tend to their heart
And hold them with care,
Just as You do for us.

Psalm 27:1; Matthew 10:29-31

PART FIVE

Prayers for the Parenting Journey

WHEN I WAS NINE MONTHS PREGNANT with my youngest son, I'd waddle into our living room and collapse into a heap of exhaustion on the couch. Kicking up my swollen feet, I'd rest my three-month-old daughter Eliza on my growing bump, where she'd snuggle in and we'd both fight back sleep as a preschooler and a kindergartener played around us.

I always like to watch people's faces when I tell them I was nine months pregnant with a newborn.

The knitting together of my family has been beautiful and heartbreaking, wild and sweet. Eliza's path to being my daughter took her across state lines and bloodlines, through temporary care, and finally, permanently into our family through adoption.

My parenting journey has been marked by surprising joys and unexpected disappointments. I'm sure yours has too.

As I prepared for our fourth child, an artist friend sent me a shirt she had made. On the front it read, "Motherhood is sanctifying." After our son was born, I stood in front of our small-town church, wearing the shirt. I held a swaddled baby in each arm and hoped my husband could capture a picture before I ended up covered in spit-up.

Parenting is *definitely* sanctifying.

I'm in a different stage of parenting now, but through the varied seasons of life together, I've learned even more about myself as I walk with my children. I see parts of me I wish weren't there—my proclivity to lose my temper and slam the door in frustration, for example. When I was a kid, I remember my dad getting upset about something. He yelled and, in his anger, threw a box of Band-Aids off a table. I watched wide eyed as little paper bandages fluttered through the air, twisting and twirling like the winged helicopter seeds from our backyard maple tree.

I don't remember what he was frustrated about, but I do remember that after he cooled off, he came into my room, sat on the edge of my bed, and apologized. Hearing a parent say "I'm sorry" has had a profound impact on the way I interact with my kids. I don't always get it right, but I try to be intentional about asking for their forgiveness. Parenting isn't just sanctifying; it's humbling, heartbreaking, and healing all at once.

I wonder what it was like for Mary and Joseph to embark on their parenting journey—a journey that surely highlighted awestruck wonderings and deep-seated fears as they welcomed a tiny baby into a weary world. What was God doing? Why them? Why now? Why couldn't they even find a place indoors for Mary to give birth?

We have plenty of questions of our own. We don't have all the answers, but just as the Israelites had a pillar of fire by night to light the way in the darkness (see Exodus 13:21), we, too, have a God who provides warmth and light for all time. This is true for the times we (or our children) have gotten it right and for the times we (or our children) most certainly haven't. For the times we feel lonely and adrift, and for the times we feel we may never get to be alone again. As we walk this path of parenting, we don't often get to see much beyond what's right in front of us. In the overwhelm and the unknowns of life together, we have to trust that God will illuminate the path and give us what we need for the day. And we cling to that stubborn hope that in the end, the light shines in the darkness—and the darkness has not overcome it (see John 1:5).

When an angel visited Mary and told her the life-shattering news of her sacred pregnancy, Mary's first act of parenting Jesus was to pray (see Luke 1:46-55). Like Mary, we can turn to God in moments of worship and awe—and in moments of unknowing, too. All these prayers matter in cosmic, eternal ways we can't begin to fathom.

The liturgies in this section hold up a broad range of what it is to ask God to guide us when parenting is honestly just overwhelming. What do you pray when your child has been bullied—or when your child has been the one perpetuating harm? What do you pray when you're holding the many tensions of parenting a child in foster care or when you're not sure how to navigate the complicated feelings of your teen?

Theologian Walter Brueggemann puts it this way: "Prayer is an act of openness to the One who sits on the throne of mercy. When we pray, we participate in the ultimate practice of humanness as we yield to a Power greater than ourselves. Our best prayers engage in candor about our lives, practice vulnerability, run risks, and rest in confident trust."[3]

When the words to pray are hard to come by and you find yourself collapsing on the couch, may these prayers light the way in your parenting journey.

A Prayer for Hearing God

O God, let us hear You
In the hot, salty tears of an upset toddler
And in the deafening door slam of
    a frustrated teen.
Help us listen, Lord, for our lives are
    loud
And parenting is overwhelming.
We can barely hear ourselves think,
Let alone process the latest headline.

O God, let us hear You
With a willingness to understand
Instead of demands to be understood.
Help us listen, Lord, to the hurting
In our families and friends,
And in our neighbors and nations, too.

O God, let us hear You.
Help us be brave enough to get quiet,
To sit with the hidden corners of our
    own hearts.
Lord, we post and shout, demanding to
    be heard,
Because we're too afraid of what we'll
    hear if we stop.

O God, let us hear You
In the cries of our children
And the cries of our neighbors.

Help us to stop talking so we may hear
What You have to tell us
Through the heartbeat of another.
O God, let us hear You.

1 Samuel 3:1-10; John 10:27; Matthew 6:6-8

A Prayer for Self-Doubt

O God, how can we possibly
Parent in these times?
How can we raise children
To love You and love others
When we are barely hanging on ourselves?

O God, we need Your help.
Meet us here in our humanity,
For Your power is made perfect in
     weakness.
And may the gentleness we give ourselves
Pour out in our interactions
With our children
And our world.

O God, we need Your help
In the wondering if we're not enough—
Not wise or patient enough,
Not kind or creative enough.
Remind us that Your grace is enough.
We feel like we're not enough,
But we know in our weakness
You are made strong.
We come to You
Like a child comes to a father,
And ask for Your help.

O God, we need Your help.
Breathe in us new life when we're weary

And courage when we're scared.
When we make mistakes, help us repair
     them,
And help us be gentle with ourselves
As we strive to be gentle with our
     children,
For You are gentle with us.

O God, we need Your help.
As we parent, help us do the next right
     thing.
Help us do the best we can with what
     we have.
Help us keep walking Your paths of peace
And righteousness.
Help us rest when we need it.
And we need it, Lord—
We really need it.

O God, we need Your help.
We don't know how to hold
The weight of expectations,
And we feel our limitations
As we navigate the pressures of parenting.

O God, we need Your help.
Help us remember we're not alone in our
     suffering.
Help us find a community of others
To raise our children with
So that we may lift each other.
For parenting was never meant
To happen in isolation,
And no parent is an island.

O God, we need Your help.
We know this season requires sacrifice.
Help us be gentle with ourselves.
We ache to pour out compassion on our
    children,
And yet we forget to be compassionate
    with ourselves.
You call us Your beloved—
Your very own children—
And we cast our shortcomings onto You,
For You care for us.

O God, we need Your help.

───────────────
Psalm 54:4; 2 Corinthians 12:9

Help us be gentle
with ourselves as
we strive to be
gentle with our
children, for You
are gentle with us.

A Prayer for the Overwhelmed

O God, help us resist the lie that we
  are alone
In the swirl of parenting, in the world
  at large.
For You hold our children, and indeed
  all of us,
In the palm of Your hand.

O God, as we stay awake at night,
Wondering how we will make it through
  another week,
Wondering what our children's lives will
  look like in the future,
Give us peace and breathe empathy
  into us,
For the need is all around us.

O God, help us to focus on right now,
Even in our exhaustion,
In our frustration,
And in our loneliness.
Help us be awake to You in the world—
In the form of a crying baby in our arms
Or a child in need of help with schoolwork
Or a hungry neighbor on the corner.

O God, we don't have to tell You
That we live in a reality with so much need,
Both in our homes

And in our broader communities,
And it's easy to feel like whatever we do
Is just a pebble in the ocean.

O God, remind us that You are present
To each individual heart
And every communal cry.
Give us strength for the day
And bright hope for tomorrow.

Psalm 46; Galatians 6:9-10

A Prayer for the Anger We Hold

O God, we are angry.
We are tired and frustrated with
    the world,
With others, and even with ourselves.

Help us know when to flip tables
And when to step away and limp
    to You.
Like a loving parent,
You welcome us into Your arms.
We scream and beat our fists into
    Your chest,
And still You hold us,
Your love stretched wide and tight
    around us.

O God, if sad looks like mad,
We are weeping under every scream.
And sometimes this current flows into
    our homes
And onto those we love, even our
    children.

Help us discern righteous anger
From our own personal rage,
So that our anger will teach us
But not control us.
Help us acknowledge our anger
But not dwell in it,

So that our anger will lead us
Into healing instead of into harm.

Give us wisdom and peace, O God,
As we give our fire to You.

Matthew 21:12-13; James 1:19-20

95

A Prayer for When We've Gotten It Wrong

O heavenly Father,
We see so clearly
The mistakes we've made
In our parenting journeys—
Even the ways we have fallen short just
    today.

In the exhaustion, we have been too tired
    to engage.
In the frustration, we have taken our
    grown-up anger
Out on our families.
In the overwhelm, we have fallen short
Of being the mothers and fathers
Our children deserve.

O Lord, with Your Abba-Father love
And the wings of a mother hen,
You welcome us as Your sons and
    daughters.
We come to You feeling like a child
In need of direction
So that we may protect and nurture
    our own.

In our exhaustion, will You renew our
    spirits?
For in taking care of our bodies and souls,
We may be filled up to tend others.

In our frustration, will You repair our
    patience?
For in gaining peace and perspective,
We may find new ways to love our
    children.

In our overwhelm, will You redeem our
    energy?
For in prioritizing where we spend our
    thoughts and time,
We may better know how to engage with
    our children.

We wish our kids came with instructions,
    O God,
Because we are improvising here—
And we're not sure the tune is right.

When we have done harm
With our presence or with our absence,
Give us tender hearts to apologize—
When we have shouted,
When we have snapped,
When we have forgotten,
When we have projected,
When we have failed.

We know that how we parent
Holds a mirror up to who we are,
And sometimes we don't like who we see.
Help us, Lord, to forgive ourselves.
Help us to see ourselves as Your beloved.
Help us to see our children as Your
    beloved too.

You are the maker of families
And the Redeemer making all things
    new.
Help us in our small choices and big
    decisions.
Give us mercy and grace—
And hearts to receive.
May we find parenting to be a mutual act
Of giving and receiving.
Forgive us for the ways we have failed,
And repair relationships we fear
Are too broken to be restored.

Fill us with true humility rooted
In Your merciful, just Spirit,
And lead us to growth
So that we may heal
That which was harmed or lost.

Our children are watching, O God.
Let us model forgiveness.
Let us say "I'm sorry" and mean it.
And may we learn to forgive ourselves.

We come to You
And lay out the tiny pebbles and great
    boulders
Of our parenting mistakes.
Help us lift off these burdens,
Repair the damage,
Learn from them what we can,
And cast them into the ocean,
Our sins seen no longer
And no longer worn around our necks.

O God of redemption,
Thank You that You have given us the gift
    of parenting,
Even in our imperfections.
You continually choose the misfits,
The stumblers, and the inexperienced
To do mighty things—to love boldly and
    care deeply.

May we learn again and again
What it is to be human—
And in our lack,
May we find Your great comfort.
In our weakness,
May we find refuge in Your wings.
And may our propensity to get it wrong
Grow in us compassion, mercy, and grace
For when others fall,
Especially our children.

You are the God of new beginnings
And fresh starts.
We lay our shame at Your feet.
And though we know we will mess up
    again,
We are always welcomed into
Your loving arms.

Romans 8:15; Luke 13:34; 1 John 1:9

May we learn
again and again
what it is to
be human—
and in our lack,
may we find
Your great
comfort.

A Prayer for When Your Child Has Broken Trust

We don't want to believe
Our child is capable of inflicting pain
Through lies or other choices.
But we know this is what it is to be
    human.
To be fully alive is to take wrong turns,
To choose the wrong door,
And even to inflict hurt or harm on
    another,
With what is said
Or left unsaid.

We pray for reconciliation—
For what is broken to be repaired,
Like the teddy bear we mended long ago,
Sewing the seams
To make it stronger.

Help our child learn from this,
Sitting in remorse but not weighed down
    by shame.
Help [child's name] return to their heart
And return to Your love.
God, not one person
Is ever too far away
That Your light can't find them.

In whatever choices were made—
Words used, actions taken,
Help us parent in each moment
With compassion and care.
Through Christ alone,
Restore that which was harmed.
Heal what has been broken.
And may we have the foresight to know
When to step away.

Give us wisdom and patience,
Compassion and gentleness.
Help us in this moment
To teach as You'd have us teach,
Love as You'd have us love.

Where hearts are hardened,
Will You soften them?
Where feelings are hurt,
Will You repair bonds?
Where trust was broken,
Will You heal the wound?
Where regrets were made
(Or perhaps there's no remorse at all),
Will You bring holy conviction?

Help us remember that we cannot
    control
Each decision our child makes.
We pray that truth would flood any lies
Believed or harbored in our family's
    hearts.

Give us wisdom
When situations arise
That we never expected—
A lie that breaks our hearts,
Reverberates through our home.

God, You hold this family in Your hands.
Help us release what is not ours to hold
So we can give all our hearts
And all the brokenness
To You.

Luke 17:3-4; Ephesians 4:25

A Prayer for One Who Parents Alone

Ever-present God,
Remind us that You are near
In our single parenting.
For we are spread thin,
Stretching to fill many roles,
And we come to You
Aware of our family's need
To be filled with Your care and great
    compassion.

O Lord, we feel like we're doing
So much for our families,
Yet it's never enough.
Today we give all we hold
And all we juggle
And all we try to balance
To You, for Your love
Is big enough for it all.
And You never abandon,
Never leave,
And never give up.

Help us when we need it—
Through rest,
Through community,
Through grace for ourselves
And our children—
When there's not enough time in the day
Or energy in our minds and bodies.

Be with us in the brimming schedules
And stacks of expectations
That weigh heavy on our hearts.
Help us see You
In our homes,
In our workplaces,
In our dreams,
In our decisions that must be made,
And in our disappointments, too.

We want the world for our children.
We want them to live freely and lightly,
Without any extra weight—
Especially weight caused by us.

Your love is extravagant,
And we ask that You will
Lavish Your love
In the corners we cannot reach,
In the expectations we cannot meet,
In the itches we cannot scratch.

We ask You to guide our paths
When school events
Like "Muffins with Moms"
Or "Donuts with Dads"
Pop up on our calendars.
Be near in the reminder
That You see our kids
And You're with us
When long days stretch into sleepless
    nights
And we wonder where You are.

We ask for endurance
In this race.
Thank You for the gift of together—
For the laughs,
For the memories made.
Meet us in it all,
And guide us in this journey.
Amen.

_____

Psalm 103:13; Hebrews 12:1

Your love is
extravagant, and
we ask that You
will lavish Your love
in the corners we
cannot reach, in
the expectations
we cannot meet.

A Prayer for Foster Parents

O God who is present
In every joy and every sorrow,
We come to You as we pray for all
Whose lives have been touched by
    foster care.

Help us see the world
And the people in it
As You do, O Lord.
Give us compassion, grace, and
    understanding
When it's easier to judge,
When we're inclined to critique,
When we cannot imagine the *hows*
    and *whys*.

For the babies, for the children,
    for the teens
All too young to understand
The hurt and harm done
By people or by systems—
Or probably both—
We pray for those
Who have received the message
That they must grow up too soon,
Those who have had connection
And safety
And all they've ever known
Stolen from them.

Lord, bring wholeness
In the wake of trauma that has occurred,
In the midst of case files
And social workers and late-night calls.
We pray for eyes that have seen too much.
We pray for hearts that have been too
    hurt.
We pray for bodies that keep the score
Of trauma, absorbing waves of pain.
We lay every expectation at Your feet
Of what this chapter may look like.
Help us see ourselves not as saviors
But as a soft place to land.
We pray that our home would be
A place of welcome and of warmth.
We pray we would give just the right
    amount
Of structure and nurture
For each and every body and soul
That comes through our door.

Lord, help us live with open hands and
    soft hearts.
We're afraid of the vulnerability that
    comes
When we throw wide the gates to love.
Help us stay soft
And forge bonds
And love with abandon.
Help us lay our protective armor at
    Your feet,
For we know we are not here for the
    whole book
But for the chapters we're part of.

We want to be brave enough to write love
And keep writing it.
Give us strength to connect,
Even if our time together is fleeting.
We know Your presence is permanent
And Your grace is enough.

For the parents these children leave,
    we pray.
We know a few lines in a file,
But we can never know the full story,
For we have not lived it—
The traumas and tragedies,
The laughter and love.
It is all part of who these children are
And where they find themselves.

We pray for healing and wholeness.
What a privilege it is to love another.
Help us accept this invitation
And understand the depth of this role
As foster parents.
Go before these children,
These families,
Our family.
Go before our hearts
And the hearts of our family.

May we form connections and
    attachments.
May we heal when the sting of loss
Feels like too much to bear.
Give us empathy and compassion;
Give us patience and humility

As we enter into brokenness.
May we see our own brokenness
And need for You, O Lord.

May our home be a place for respite
    and rest.
May our time together be marked by
Healing in the hard places.
May the heaviness
Of what has brought us together not
    overshadow
Laughter and joy and memories that last.

Lord, help us trust You,
Even when Your ways leave us confused
And our hearts battered.
You are our Protector and Provider,
And we pray that You would go with
    the children
Who are with us for only a season.

Give us all peace
When the wind and waves shake us.
Help us still believe that You are walking
    on water
And that You will never leave any of us.

Help us be consistent.
Breathe life into us for each new day,
Because healing takes time.

Give us perspective to recognize our
    privilege
As we enter into the pain and beauty
Of sharing life together.

Help us welcome with warmth,
And when our time together ends,

May we go with grace.

Help these children be brave enough to
    receive love
And courageous enough to give it too.
Be near to them in their fear.
In the inconsistencies, be a constant.
In the hard goodbyes, be a comfort.

Thank You for stories that converge
And take our hearts to new places.
Help us honor both our own stories
And the stories of these children
And their families.

We pray for the children already in
    our family
And the new ways they will share
Their home and the people in it.
Help them be patient and kind
And know that Your love never fails.
Help us prepare their hearts
As we prepare room,
And give us words
As we stumble through hard
    conversations.

O God, You are the author of life.
You write brilliant stories,
And we know that we may never see how
All these plot twists and tangles
Will come together for good.

Help us be in the messy middle of
    humanity.

Redeem these systems.
Make families whole.
Protect the vulnerable.
Set captives free.
Thank You for Your steadfast love
That does not come and go as the winds
    change.

Psalm 86:15; Ephesians 2

Give us all peace
when the wind and
waves shake us. Help
us still believe that
You are walking on
water and that You will
never leave any of us.

A Prayer for When Your Child Has Been Bullied

O God, defender of the suffering,
We are heartbroken as we hold our
    child's
Battered heart in our hands.

We cry out against the mistreatment,
Against the lies and the pain inflicted
On their heart and mind, body and soul.

We grieve with them,
For humans, even the youngest among us,
Can be so cruel,
And we weep with them
As they hurt.

Be with us as we put back together
That which was broken.
Be with us in their tears
And in ours, too.

This is not as it should be, Lord—
Cruel comments and the sting of
    schoolyard bullies.
We know that hurting hearts hurt others,
And yet right now we struggle to find
    compassion
For the perpetrator of such harm.

Teach us Your ways, O Lord.
Give us space for the emotions to breathe
So our wounds may heal.

God, help us not to return violence of
    words or actions
With more violence.
Instill in our child their worthiness.
Help us remind them of their belovedness
As our child and Yours.

Help them understand that bullying
    says much
About the oppressor
And nothing about our child.
Help them see their differences as
    beautiful,
For they are uniquely and wonderfully
    made.
Give them safe spaces to play and to learn.
Give them friends who love them as
    they are.
Give them adults to watch over and
    intervene when necessary.
Give them comfort and peace.
Provide healing and rest.
And remove every ounce of shame,
Because we know this is not of You.

O Jesus, Man of Sorrows,
We know You understand intimately
What it is to be mocked, maligned, and
    mistreated.

God, we know deep hurt will not
    disappear in one day.
And we know that in each of us
Is the propensity to hurt another
And hurt You.
While there is no silver lining to these
    dark clouds,
May this incident act as a reminder
To be empathetic and compassionate
To those on the margins—
The hurting and the oppressed.

May You forge paths of wholeness
When the time comes for repentance
By those who have done harm.
Move us toward relationship and
    reconciliation.

And when that is not to be,
May our child know
It is not their fault.

Heal us, O Lord.
We come to You with broken hearts—
Both ours and our child's.
We know You will hold them
With the tender love of a parent.

_____

Isaiah 53:3; Psalm 9:9; Isaiah 1:17

A Prayer for When Your Child Bullies Another

O God, lover of the oppressor
As well as the victim,
Compassionate toward those who are hurt
As well as those who harm,
Merciful toward the afflicted
As well as those who inflict,
We come to You with fractured hearts,
For our child has perpetuated harm,
And we aren't sure what to do
Or what to say.

In this moment, we need eyes
To see our child's heart.
And we pray that the way
We approach this situation
Would not harm or hurt
Or heap more shame
On their soul.

We have seen much goodness in our child,
And now we must grapple with
The pain of what it is
To fully be human,
Not immune to causing harm to another.

Create in our child a spirit of lament
As we talk with them about their words
    and actions.

Help us listen, and help us guard against
    judgment.
Help us look for the feelings in what they
    show us,
And may we sit in those feelings with
    them.

Let us pay attention to the feelings behind
What they have said or done to harm
    another,
For we know it's often when we hurt
That we are most prone to hurt another.

Help this conflict sharpen our ability
To love our child well in this moment,
And may they feel that love in return.

Help us to forgive our child's
    transgressions
As You forgive ours.
And help us to guide our child
Through their apologies.
May they be empowered to express remorse
With sincerity and compassion
And admit responsibility
When they've been wrong.
May they make amends,
Express repentance,
And make reparations
With our guidance.

Give them ears to listen
To how their words and actions
Have harmed another.

May we always model what it is
To apologize to others
With empathy and grace
So that our children will know that
Apologies are part of what it means
For all of us to be human.

God, parenting is difficult,
And we wish we had all the answers.
But we know we don't have to,
And what we do have
Is access to a well that won't run dry.

May we drink of the Living Water
And open our arms wide
To our child as they get lost
And find their way again.

You are the God of fresh starts,
New beginnings,
And a million second chances;
The God of liberation from past mistakes;
The God of forgiveness.
Thank You for always pointing us
Toward love,
Even when we lose our way.

_____

Matthew 6:12; 1 John 1:9

PART SIX

Prayers for Nurturing Faith and Character

TWICE A YEAR, my husband and I attend parent-teacher conferences. The teachers send home report cards prior to the meetings, and before we pull up to the school, I make sure to flip through the kids' folders of drawings, essays, and test scores. But when we ask our kids what we should expect when we walk through the classroom door and wiggle into the too-small chairs to talk with their teachers, we're not talking about assessments and homework. We're talking about their character.

We care more about *who* they are than *what* they accomplish.

While I deeply desire for my kids to be lifelong learners and to try their best in all they do, their integrity, empathy, and compassion matter more to me than any standardized test score.

When I think about my son's first-grade conferences, I don't remember how many addition and subtraction facts he memorized, but I *do* remember hearing that he kept an eye out for anyone who sat on the playground "buddy bench." When a student was feeling left out at recess, they could sit on the bench to signal to others that they could use a friend. As I heard my son's teacher share about how he eagerly widened his playground circle to include the lonely, I learned more about his character than a report card could ever reflect.

I find myself praying less about the success my kids achieve in the eyes of the world and more for the fruit of the Spirit to grow in their lives. My kids love to blurt out an old Sunday school song that says, "The fruit of the Spirit is *not a watermelon!*" Even as they get older, they love filling in the blank with all sorts of fruit: strawberry, mango, banana. The catchy tune then shares what the fruit of the Spirit *actually* is: love, joy, peace, patience, kindness, goodness, faithfulness, gentleness, and self-control (see Galatians 5:22-23).

This truth reorients me to the true markings of life in Christ. What a refreshing reminder that my worth is wrapped up not in what I achieve but in who I am in God's cosmic knowing. When I untangle myself from what the world deems worthy, I can see with new eyes what is truly important in my life—and in my hopes and longings for my children, too.

In the New Testament we read about Timothy's ministry. When I think about nurturing faith and character in children, two names that come to mind are Lois and Eunice—Timothy's grandmother and mother. Their lives had eternal reverberations, greatly influencing Timothy's life in Christ. In fact, Paul underlined this familial foundation in a letter to him: "I remember your genuine faith, for you share the faith that first filled your grandmother Lois and your mother, Eunice. And I know that same faith continues strong in you" (2 Timothy 1:5, NLT).

This doesn't mean that Timothy was flawless—he had struggles and pain points in his life just like the rest of us. But when the winds of adversity surrounded him, he had a strong foundation in the love of God, built by his family.

I have no doubt that the women who raised Timothy prayed for the boy he was and the man he became. Their faithfulness cultivated a Christlike character at an early age (see 2 Timothy 3:15). As a mentor, Paul taught and encouraged young Timothy, "Don't let anyone look down on you because you are young, but set an example for the believers in speech, in conduct, in love, in faith and in purity" (1 Timothy 4:12).

As we know, no child or parent is perfect. But when we learn of the seemingly small acts of faithfulness, like the unexpected mercy of a child extending playground friendship, we catch a glimmer of our prayers being answered in the lives of our children. And we see who we—and our children——are truly called to be in Christ. What a relief it is that grace is freely given (see Ephesians 1:6), no tests required.

May this section of prayers and liturgies help you invite God into the cries of your heart for your child's character. From asking for God to guide them on their faith journey to turning to the Spirit for holy help in raising families that resist the lure of consumerism, the following prayers are for nourishing your child's inner life. And perhaps you'll find yourself being filled and transformed in new ways too.

A Prayer for Following the Way of Jesus

O God, we want to raise children
Who know they are loved
By their Creator
With a love so big
It would take a lifetime
To swim in the ocean of Your grace—
And even then
It wouldn't be enough.

We want our children to know,
Even as they stumble and fall,
That they reflect the image of God:
Created and known and loved.
We pray that they would know You
As an anchor to their souls.
May they know Your love,
A love big enough to absorb it all—
Every question, every doubt, every fear.
For in Jesus Christ,
Sin has been wiped clean,
And we have been made whole.

Give our children comfort when they feel
    most alone.
Give them courage when they need to
    stand for what's right.
Give them compassion when they meet
    someone in need of mercy.

Thank You for the faith of a child,
For the open, tender heart
That many of us grown-ups lose as years
    go by.
Let us point to You
In the comings and goings of the day.
Spirit, guide us
As we navigate the groans of creation.

O Lord, we thank You for grace freely
    given,
For mercy poured out,
For infinite second chances,
Even in our imperfections and doubts.
We pray our children
Would see in us a faith
That draws them in and toward You.
Lord of small things,
Give us all the faith of a mustard seed,
For we know that's all it takes to move
    mountains—
The mountains that bow down
Before Your majesty.

Where You are, peace is.
And You are all around our children.
Spirit, hover over little hearts and minds.
Go before them.
Lead them, guide them, whisper into
    their hearts
That they are safe in the arms of Christ.

Lord, You said let the little children come,
And we give our children to You.

May they ask questions
With no easy answers,
And may we be rooted in You,
Firm enough in our foundations
To sit in the mystery with them.
Help us learn together.
Bring us into Your living Word,
And awaken us to Your truth,
O Word that became flesh.

May we honor the humanity
Of our children.
May we remember You are always in
    pursuit.
May we point our children to You
In times of great rejoicing and deep sorrow.
For as long as we have the gift
Of guiding them on this earth,
Walking them home to You,
May they see You in every star
And every cloud.
May they feel You in the breeze
And in the dirt under their feet.

God of rescue and restoration,
Be near in the raising up of this child.
May they walk in Your Spirit
And follow Your paths of peace.
May they worship You with their words
And deeds.
May they join in the ancient truths of
    Your great love.
May they call on Your name.
Thank You for the ways

You have revealed Yourself to our
    children,
And we ask that You would continue
    to do so.
May [child's name]'s life
Be an outpouring of Your love.

Help them seek first Your Kingdom.
May they believe in their bones
That You'll provide what they need.

Help them to be true to themselves
And to You, Lord, in every way.
May they proclaim You, O Christ,
In all they do and all they are.
May they listen to Your words, Lord Jesus,
For these words are our map on how
    to live.

Thank You, Lord.
We praise You,
For You are never far from our children
Or from us.

_John 14:6; Hebrews 10:23; 2 Timothy 4:18; Romans 10:4;
Psalm 119:105_

A Prayer for a Grateful Spirit

O God, giver of good gifts,
Big and small,
We give thanks
For the honor
And the privilege
Of being a parent.

We give thanks, O God,
For laughter around the table
And for arms around each other.
We give thanks, O God,
For shoulders to cry on
And hands to hold.

O God, giver of good gifts,
We praise You
And thank You
For Your mercies,
New each morning,
Even when the mercies are hard to see.

We give thanks, O God,
For memories made
And for hope in what is to come.
We give thanks, O God,
For the quiet evenings
And the chaotic mornings too.

O God, giver of good gifts,
All we are
And hope to be,
We offer to You
In thanksgiving for this life together.

We give thanks, O God,
For squishy babies
And curious toddlers.
We give thanks, O God,
For growing kids
And teens who are finding their own way
And young adults who are becoming
    more themselves.

O God, giver of good gifts,
Thank You for moments of time
When heaven meets earth
In the form of dance parties
And bedtime stories,
Reheated leftovers
And making the team.

We give thanks, O God,
For inside jokes
And knowing looks.
We give thanks, O God,
For love freely given
And love freely received.

For all things,
Big and small,
We give thanks, O God.

James 1:17; Lamentations 3:22-23; 1 Corinthians 2:12; Psalm 100

We give thanks,
O God, for laughter
around the table
and for arms around
each other. We give
thanks, O God,
for shoulders to cry
on and hands
to hold.

A Prayer for a Creative Spirit

O Maker God,
We marvel
And sometimes scratch our heads
At these magnificent children
And the magical ways
They view the world.

O Maker God,
Help us empower our children
To be cocreators with You.
Help us encourage our children
To mix new paints and beat new drums,
Introducing us to colors and songs
We never knew before.

O Maker God,
Help us experience You
In the ways our children imagine life.
Let us see You in what they make
And in how they make it
And in how they beam
When they say,
"It is good."

O Maker God,
Let us celebrate our children's creative lives
By saying yes more often,
Entering into the mess,
And meeting You in new ways.

O Maker God,
We know someday
We won't find paper-towel-roll creations
And caps off markers
And drumsticks and scattered sheet music
On the floor.

O Maker God,
May our children
Know what it is to blaze their own trail,
To go their own way,
And to create something entirely new,
Hand in hand
With You.

Isaiah 64:8; 1 Samuel 18:6; Ephesians 2:10; Revelation 4:11

A Prayer for Dirty Hands

We pray for the small, sticky hands
And the fingerprints they leave behind
With each intricate swirl.
May they know the care of their Creator,
And may we remember it too.

As we gather at the sink
To rinse tiny, soapy palms,
We thank You for fresh water.
Cleanse our hearts,
For we lament that some children in
    our midst
Lack clean water and helping hands.
Cleanse our hearts,
For we lament that we haven't seen
These little ones as our own.

Unfurl our fists and open our hands,
Because You are living water
For all Your children.

Isaiah 44:3; Psalm 51:10; Proverbs 4:23; John 4:14

A Prayer for a Child with Big Feelings

O Lord, tune our hearts
So that we may be perceptive to our child
As they process the complicated world
    around them.
Help us guide humbly
Without needing every right answer.
Help us speak honestly
Without flooding them with information.

O Lord, lead us as we open our arms
To bring our little one and their big
    feelings close.
For they have picked up our grown-up
    worries
And worn them as their own,
Mirroring our own furrowed brows and
    tight shoulders
After hearing bits of a hushed
    conversation
Or catching a headline not meant for
    the young.

In our child's confusion,
May we be a safe place to land.
In our child's anger,
May we have the wisdom to help them
    process.
In our child's sadness,
May we create a space for listening.

In our child's anxieties,
May we help them find ways to heal.

O Christ, who welcomed little children
In their full humanity,
Grant us compassion and connectivity,
Empathy and endurance
As we walk with our child
Toward Your great love.

_____

Deuteronomy 31:8; Zephaniah 3:17

Grant us
compassion and
connectivity,
empathy and
endurance as
we walk with
our child toward
Your great love.

A Prayer for Consumerism

O God of abundance,
We come to You and ask
For Your Holy guidance
As we raise children
In a culture shouting and selling
Promises of more.

You have given us what we need for
    this day,
And yet we confess that our own lives
Have been marked by want.
Forgive us for stumbling into greed,
For biting into the fruit of consumerism,
And for fighting for a life marked by
    scarcity
Instead of gratitude for Your abundance.

O Lord, how do we raise children
Who are not led by our culture's values
About what we consume
And how much of it we consume
And how fast we can consume it?

We have bought the lie
That more will fill us,
That new will sustain us,
That big will protect us.

We have even commodified You, O Lord,
Thinking that if we do

Or say the right things,
We can buy Your love—
A love that is given freely
And never for sale.

We have fallen into the trap of entitlement.
Enlighten us and rescue us
From the dark allure of more.

We have reasoned and rationalized
The ways we spend our money,
Forgetting that all we have is Yours.
We have fallen asleep
To the truth that how we spend our money
Is how we spend our lives.
And in our hunt for more,
We have become the prey.
We have conflated bigger, newer houses
With security and success,
And our children are watching.

We have told our little ones
To give to the poor,
But we have stored our own treasures
In 401(k)s and savings accounts.
We have replaced our identity as Your
    children
With crowns of privilege
And robes of prestige.

How can we raise children to value
Your Son, Jesus Christ,
When we have filled our hearts
With a search for more
Instead of a search for You?

O Lord, we lament the ways
We have taken the lie of the enemy
And eaten it whole.
Deliver us from the depth of our greed,
And free us from the clutches of the
    evil one.

Forgive us for the ways we have evangelized
The gospel of consumerism,
And deliver us from the ways
We have worshiped at the altar
Of consumption.

You have given us our daily bread,
Yet we have desired the whole bakery.
We have eaten until we are full,
And yet we have forgotten our hungry
    neighbor.

Convict us, Spirit, of the ways we have
    filled ourselves
With everything but Your goodness.
Fill the voids we have with Your tender
    mercies
And gifts of grace.

We ask for self-control as we are bombarded
By messaging all around us
That tells us to keep climbing,
Keep collecting,
Keep growing.

What have You required of us, O Lord?
To act justly, to love mercy, to walk
    humbly

With You.
Forgive us when we have forgotten this,
And walk beside us as our children watch
Our journey of a life lived with You.

We have built sandcastles
And called them good,
And we have lost our footing
When the waves of life crashed down.
We have cared more about what we have
Than who You are.
We have been so focused
On shiny objects that we have neglected
To see the treasure of You
In the person across from us.

Let Your Word be more than
Sunday school platitudes,
And may we be transformed
By the shackle-breaking, liberating,
    glorious love
Of Jesus Christ,
Who breaks chains of consumerism
And rescues us from the pit of
    entitlement.

If we have abundance,
Let it be an abundance of peace.
If we have wealth,
Let it be the wealth of memories
    together.
If we must consume,
Let us consume Your Word.
If we must invest,
Let it be in the poor.

If we have more than we need,
Let us give more freely.

When we look to our children, remind us
That You are the giver of good gifts
And You are a compassionate God
Who never stops seeking us, pursuing us,
And welcoming us home,
Even when we have fallen short.

Help us live with hands open
So that we may receive Your abundant life.
Help us raise children to walk paths
Of generosity rooted in Your great love.

We thank You, O Lord,
For what You have given us.
And while we lament our inclinations to
    excess,
We also ask for Your guidance
To raise families in gospel generosity
And lavish love.
Keep us far from the enemy's snare
Of newer, bigger, and better.
For Yours is the Kingdom,
The house upon the rock,
And the very Rock itself.
Amen.

Hebrews 13:5-6; Micah 6:8; Matthew 7:24-27; Matthew 13:45-46;
Matthew 7:11; John 10:10; Deuteronomy 32:4

A Prayer for Media Consumption

O God of the galaxies,
Our world has grown at light speed
And become smaller by the second.
At our fingertips, we have access
To millions of points
Of education and entertainment,
Connectivity and consumption.

We pray for wisdom
Over what our children consume
And how they consume it.
Help us not to be afraid of media
Nor entranced by it.

Protect our children's growing minds
    and hearts
From the dark corners of the internet
And from the lies of the enemy,
Who seeks to steal and destroy.

Protect our children from streams of
    temptation
And from the lure of right now,
For we know what they read and see and
    do online
Has lasting reverberations in who they are
And who they will be.
Help us use the screens in front of us
As tools of healing, not harm.
Give us wisdom to neither

Weaponize nor idolize technology
But rather use it as a window to connect
    and energize
For justice and for truth.
May technology be a gateway to spread
    messages
Of hope and not hate.
May technology bridge divides
And sow reparations instead of disrepair.

Help us learn to navigate the digital tools
    we have in front of us
So that we may beat our swords of
    technology
Into plowshares of peace.
Help our children have the discernment
    to know
That seeing online is not always believing.
Protect them from worlds of excess at
    their fingertips,
And guard them against the ever-present
    lure of a glowing screen.
Keep our children from falling prey to
    online bullying.
May our children be neither the victims
Nor the perpetrators in these attacks,
And shield them from the traps of
    comparison
And the pressure to commodify themselves,
To contort into an image morphed by
    filters and smoke screens.

Help us to keep the good in what
Decades of brilliant minds have
    illuminated for us

In our technology.
We lament that we, too, can lose our sense
    of time and place,
Transporting ourselves into digital worlds
Because our current reality
Is much too painful.
Help us to have the courage to be in
    the now
Instead of escaping into a false reality.

Help us as parents to be present
And fight the desire to disconnect from
    our own reality,
For we have used screens as a way to
    numb ourselves
From the deeper ache of our hearts.
We've used screens as distractions
And cheap alternatives to true connectivity
With others and with You.
God, there are days when our children
    spend
More time with screens
Than they do with us.
And there are days when we have spent
More time with screens
Than with our children.
Lord, have mercy.
Our children have soaked in more
    messaging
Than we even know about.
Christ, have mercy.

When we have the option to play outside,
Let us opt for that instead of a video game.

When we have the option to sit with a
    friend,
Let us opt for that instead of a text.
When we have the option to explore a city,
Let us opt for that instead of a video.
When we have the option to read,
Let us opt for that instead of a movie.
When we have the option to confront
    injustice,
Let us opt for that instead of a social
    media comment.

Protect our daughters and sons from
    streaming violent or sexual content.
Guard them from falling prey to lost
    social and emotional skills.
Help us and the other adults in their lives
    live with intention
As we model healthy media behaviors,
Turning off the TV and putting away
    phones
So we may practice what we preach.

And may our children's media usage be
    a door
Into the realities of their local and global
    neighbors
That they could never see otherwise.
May their media usage grow them
In compassion, empathy, and
    understanding.
May they see the world from another's
    point of view
And see You in bigger ways because of it.

Isaiah 2:4; Colossians 3:16; Hebrews 10:23-25

A Prayer for Siblings

O God, You have given us the gift of family.
Thank You for the gift of together.
Thank You for the children
You have knit together
As brothers and sisters,
Their stories connected
And interwoven in the fabric of family.

God, we have seen our children grow
And develop their own personalities,
And we ask You to help our children
     value each other
And the gift of having someone
To journey through life with.
When they argue,
May they ask for forgiveness.
When they disappoint each other,
May they heal what was broken.
We pray that they will always defend
     each other.
May they see their sibling as a lifelong friend,
A gift of family
Connected by the thread of love.

In the common language,
In the shared experiences,
In the laughter,
In the loss,
Bring them together
So they might not grow apart as they
     grow older.

Connect them in a legacy of love
That goes beyond bloodlines.
In the sibling rivalry, give peace.
May they realize they're on the same team—
Each other's first playmate and first friend.
May they know that being together
Is a gift from You.

We want our children to be unified,
No matter the different paths their
     preferences lead them on.
May they see each other as teammates.
May they know they belong to each other.
May they make memories while they're
     young
So they can laugh at their adventures
When they themselves are crowned with
     gray.
May they be united in You.
May they be each other's defender as well
     as playmate.
Help us let each of these children know
Just how loved and valued they are.
May we never play favorites,
And may we be consistent
In reminding them
That we are a family
And we stick together
And work together
And cheer each other on.

O God, we thank You for the gift of
     brothers and sisters.

Hebrews 12:14; Hebrews 13:1

125

A Prayer for a Child's Friendship

O God of community,
We aren't meant to do life alone.
May we remember that
This sacred truth
Goes for the youngest among us too.

We pray for friendship
To be extended and received
All the days of our child's life.
May their relationships build bridges,
And may they dance across divides
To the tune of a new friend.
May their relationships broaden their
    world
And help them grow in empathy
And understanding, too.

We pray for camaraderie
That sparks wonder and joy,
Laughter and adventure
In all the ages and stages
Of our child's life.

Whether they have a group of friends
Or just one kindred spirit,
Whether the friendships last a lifetime
Or are treasured for just a season,
May our child find the kinship of
    another
Steeped in mutual merriment and respect.

Help us as parents to support our child
And trust You as we do.
Help us to encourage them
As they develop their own personality
And cultivate their own friendships
In their own ways.

Build a trusting relationship
Between us, O Lord,
So that they feel comfortable
To confide when friendship troubles arise.
And when conflicts do bubble over,
Protect their heart, O Lord.
Guard them against creating cliques,
And give them a spirit of kindness
To sow grace
Where there is misunderstanding
And hope
Where there is hurt.

Thank You, O God,
For the gift of friendship.
May all of us,
Children and grown-ups too,
Love one another
As You have loved us.

Proverbs 18:24; John 15:12-13

A Prayer for a Daughter to Know Her Worth

O God, we thank You for the gift
And the privilege of raising a daughter,
And we ask for Your help
As we walk with her
As she grows
And learns what it is
To become more the person
You made her to be.

Lord, we know our world
Does not give girls and women
The same kind of access
And opportunity
As their brothers,
Seeing a woman's worth
As pennies on the dollar.
We lament the years of oppression
And glass ceilings women have faced,
The weight of expectations placed
Like pearls around their necks.

But we know that You have
Given us imagination
To see Your Kingdom here,
To see our daughter as You
Have created her to be—
All the brilliance of humanity,
The swirls of strength and gentleness,

The brilliance of power and kindness,
The vast array of the fruit of Your Spirit
On full display.

Our daughter is watching, Lord,
What we say
And what we do.
Give us speech that is empowering and
    honoring.
Give us fathers tenderness to listen,
To fully hear what our daughter is saying.
Give us mothers confidence to talk about
    beauty and bodies
Without an ounce of shame.
Help us not cave under culture's crass
    expectations
Of filters and fillers.
Help our daughter resist the pressure
To measure her worth
By numbers on a scale.
Help her not be weighed down
By the lies of the serpent
Who whispers that she's not enough
And never will be.
Help her never feel the need
To shrink the body or gifts You have
    given her
To fit the pressures of someone else.

Help our daughter know her worth.
Ignite in her passions.
Empower her to use her mind and heart
To make this world a more compassionate
    place

For all people.
Breathe in her ways to love with creativity
And imagination for what could be.
Help her dance on top of injustice
And crush the serpent with her heel.

Give her purpose; give her peace.
Help her choose the way of love.
Help her be brave.
Help her dare to begin again.
Help her never apologize when others say
She's too much or not enough.

Help us not lock her into cells of our
     expectations,
But help us nurture and nourish her to
     be exactly who
You've created her to be.

Thank You for wildflowers and train sets.
Thank You for long division and poetry.
Thank You for tangly tresses and
     glitter glue.

God, in Your Kingdom,
The princess doesn't need rescuing,
Except by Your merciful hand.
Help us surround her with empowerment.
Help us cheer her on and make a safe place
For her to land when she's tired.
God, help her slay dragons
And stand up when something's wrong.
Help her know that the ways of Your
     Kingdom

Mean down is up
And the way out is in.
Tune her heart to You,
And whisper into the quiet places of her
     heart that
While there are a million paths she
     can take,
Her worth doesn't lie in productivity—
In what she can or can't do—
But in her value as a beloved daughter
Of the Holy One.
And what a gift it is to love her into this
     knowledge.

When the hardships come,
May she hold on to You.
When the doubts rise,
May she be buoyed by Your love.

Help her stand and shout
As she advocates for others
And for herself, too.
Help her rest,
For that, too, is holy.
Help us encourage her
And show her women who have walked
Your ways of peace and power.

We pray for the daughters
Around the world
And in our own community
Who enter a culture that teaches lies
And demeans and demoralizes Your
     daughters, Lord.

We weep for all that is lost when half
    Your Kingdom
Is told the light inside them is worth less
Than the lights of others.

Lord, let our daughter shine,
And illuminate the darkness
Of every lie told,
Even the lies in Your name,
For the gospel is one of freedom,
And You have set us free.

We lament the ways we have perpetuated
    an unjust world
For our daughter.
We cry out for the ways we have turned
    our face
From Your image in our daughter.
Help us know it's never too early
And never too late
To raise an empowered daughter
Who walks in the Spirit.

Ruth 1–4; Esther 1–10

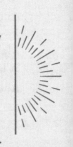

When the
hardships come,
may she hold on
to You. When the
doubts rise, may
she be buoyed
by Your love.

129

A Prayer for a Son to Walk the Way of Jesus

What is it, Lord, to be a man?
What is it to raise one?

In a context where men
Can be almost anything,
We pray for stamina
To raise a son
Who values gentleness
Over strength,
Who values peace
Over power.

Liberate us, Lord,
From the binds
Of toxic masculinity
In our home
And in our hearts.

Rescue us, O God,
From the trappings
Of celebrated violence
In our words
And in our wonderings.

Make us parents
Who welcome emotion
And tenderness.

Remind us that our child
And indeed we ourselves
Are created in Your very image.

Help us fathers
To model self-awareness,
Self-control,
And self-compassion.
For our son is watching
A world where men
Are encouraged to run
The other way.

Help us mothers
To model self-respect,
Self-empowerment,
And self-compassion.
For our son is watching
In a world where women
Are encouraged to shrink away.

We pray for our son as he grows,
Shooting up like a dandelion
After a summer rain,
His legs leaner,
His heart fertile ground.
Help us tend to his soul.
Cultivate in us a sense of awe
For Your creation.

O Creator,
For his developing brain
And body,

We ask for discernment.
Surround him with
Friends and family
Who model lives
That honor themselves
And each other.

As we peek out the window
At the oranges and pinks of a glorious
    sunset,
Help us point to You,
And help our son see the holy artist
Within himself.
Let us create with him
So he becomes a cocreator with You.

As we walk along the wooded path
Under the canopy of great oaks
Dropping acorns underfoot,
Help us point to You
And help him see the holy protector
Within himself.
Let us nurture him
So he becomes a nurturer like You.

As we take our seats on the hard plastic
Of the crowded subway,
Packed with grandmothers
And babies and college students,
Help us point to You,
And help him see the holy unity
Within Your family.

As we sit upon the shore,
Skipping a smooth stone on the resting
    water,
Help us point to You,
And help him see the holy grace
You have planted within him.

Show us how to raise
Artists and adventurers,
Thinkers and teachers,
Nurturers and navigators.
Let them run with abandon
The race set out for them.
Give them grace; give them grit,
For they're inheriting a world
That says strength means
Bigger, faster, louder;
That says winning is
Conquering, collecting, conquesting.
But perhaps we can lead them
To a Kingdom
That flips upside down
Our notions of
Power and of victory,
That points them to
The tenderness of a Shepherd,
The benevolence of a King,
The outstretched arms of a Father.

Help us listen to our son
So he will learn to listen first and speak
    slowly.

Help us cry with him
So he will learn tears are holy indicators,
Of what it is to be human.

Help us embrace him
With open arms
After foolishness
And wayward wanderings,
For You model parental mercy.

We pray for our son,
That he would be empowered
While divesting his power,
That he would honor himself
While honoring his most marginalized
    neighbor,
That he would have courage
To turn away
From the temptation of excess,
From the delight of more.

God, we are greedy in our prayers,
And still we ask for more:
For joy in our son,
For delight and for celebration,
For the holy sound of
Giggles and hearty laughs
To emanate from his
Very soul.

Our culture has not modeled well
What it is to raise a son,
What it is to be a man.
But we have hope

Because we have a heavenly Father
And a compassionate Son
And a Holy Spirit who will never
    leave us.
It is in the name of the triune God
That we raise our boy
And that we pray these things.
Amen.

———————————
Genesis 33; Titus 3:2; Matthew 6:33; James 1:22; Ephesians 6:11-12

A Prayer for Peace

May be used on International Day of Peace (September 21)

O Prince of Peace,
We come to You,
For our hearts don't feel peaceful
And our world doesn't either.

All around us, chaos swirls
Along with our emotions,
And we're trying to find our footing,
Trying to raise a family that follows You,
Even in times of upheaval—
Especially then.

We seek the peace of Your Kingdom,
And we ask You to help us
Be makers of peace too—
In our community,
In our world,
In our family,
In our hearts.

O Lord, we know that we have confused
Passive peacekeeping with active
    peacemaking.
We have sought a false peace
That doesn't ruffle feathers
And avoids conflict
Instead of the true peace
That comes in the shelter of Your wings.

Lord, we seek refuge in You.
Will You instill in us the values of Your
Upside-down Kingdom,
Where peacemakers are blessed
Even if it doesn't always feel that way?
The world is on fire,
Ignited by shouts and screams at one
    another.
Help us not add to the noise
But seek to listen.
Help us seek to understand
Instead of only trying to be understood.

When Jesus broke in,
The angels declared,
"Peace on earth
And goodwill to all."
But we have lost our way
And shut our eyes to the star leading
    the way.
We have chosen the way of self
Over the love of neighbor,
Choosing violence of word and deed
Over Your peaceable Kingdom,
Where the wolf lies down with the lamb
And a child leads us all.

God, help us work for peace
With and for our children.
Help us raise children
Who sow love instead of hate,
Planting seeds that will become
Mighty oaks of righteousness

And cultivating lives of justice
So that our world may bloom with
    Your love.
May our family be known by our love
And by our willingness to show up
And stand with those who are often
    unheard.
May we use our voices to speak
When something is wrong
Or someone is hurt.

We pray for those—locally and globally—
For whom conflict is a close companion,
For whom violence waits in the shadows,
For whom war is never far away.
We ache for the day
When warring nations will be at peace,
When brother will not fight against
    brother.

We cry out for the ways
We have hurt one another
And ask forgiveness for the times
We have not stood up for peace.

Thank You for Your Spirit,
Who dwells within us
And around us.
We ask for guidance
And for open hands and curious hearts
As we enter into challenging
    conversations.

We ask for a spirit of peace as we
Interact with our world and the people in it.

Give us a spirit of humility so that we
May have compassion for those we don't
    understand.
Give us a spirit of gentleness
So that we may have mercy for ourselves.
Give us a spirit of boldness
So that we may love.

We come to You as imperfect
    peacemakers,
Our hearts bruised and bloodied
Over well-intentioned failures.
We know we don't always get it right,
But we know this is the way of the Lord.
And we ask that in each new day
We would wake with a posture of love
And a bent toward peace.

We pray that our hopes for a more
    flourishing world
Would be renewed with Your unfailing
    mercy.
Help us rebuild and repair where harm
    has been done,
Both in our land and in our hearts.

We ask for Your peace that surpasses all
    understanding,
And that we would be emboldened
    enough to work for peace
And humble enough to turn to You again
    and again.

We lay down our swords
And our fighting words

And our deep desire to be right
As we come to You.

If we shout,
May we shout good news to the poor.
If we fight,
May we fight injustice.
If we push,
May we push doors open toward freedom.
If we wrestle,
May we wrestle with You.
If we break,
May we break the chains of captivity.
If we defend,
May we defend the vulnerable.
If we tear down,
May we tear down walls that divide.

Matthew 5:9; Luke 2:14; Isaiah 11:6; Isaiah 61:3

We pray that
our hopes for a
more flourishing
world would be
renewed with Your
unfailing mercy.

PART SEVEN

Prayers for Holidays and Holy Days

WHEN I WAS YOUNG, my jaw dropped when I learned that the word *holiday* came from *holy day*. After all, I'd heard cultural commentators warn against the danger of a store clerk bidding a shopper "Happy Holidays" instead of "Merry Christmas." With all my ten-year-old enthusiasm, I took to shouting, "Happy Holy Days!" quite frequently—and it wasn't annoying at all. Now, as a parent to a ten-year-old myself, I'm in awe of my parents' patience.

What are holy days—or Christian holidays—and what sets them apart from the rest of our yearly celebrations and days of observation? Theologies and preferences vary between Christian denominations, and so do the days set aside as holy. But we're united as one body of believers. We base our rhythms on a church calendar made up of sacred days and observations that point us to Jesus. The church year works as scaffolding, holding us together and reminding us of our unity in Christ.

As I've become more intentional about seeking God in the ordinary and extraordinary moments of parenting, I've found myself becoming more rooted to the rhythms of the church calendar, learning that these sacred seasons and days have a way of orienting us to God's time.

We know that God is the creator and keeper of time, working within the constraints of our world—and outside them. Scripture refers to time in two ways, as *chronos* and *kairos*. Chronos is where our word *chronological* comes from—it's the passing of time minute by minute. Kairos is a bit tougher to define. It's the passing of time moment by moment.

In our family, we have a kitchen calendar that organizes the comings and goings of our daily life—soccer practice, doctor's appointments, school performances. My husband and I share color-coded online schedules, and my watch is ready to remind me that I'm running late. (I usually am.)

God's time shows us a new way.

Shane Claiborne, Jonathan Wilson-Hartgrove, and Enuma Okoro, compilers of *Common Prayer*, a collection of modern liturgies, put it this way: "The church calendar does not help us remember our meetings, but it aims at nothing less than changing the way we experience time and perceive reality."[4]

If chronos is a line, kairos is a circle. Chronos is our human way to measure time, but kairos is a mind-bending way to understand a God who is both in and out of time, in and out of our world, our galaxy, our universe. Kids seem to have an imagination for this—superheroes traverse time and space, and timelines are rarely chronological. And as my seven-year-old recently told me when we were playing with action figures, "This guy is from another dimension."

Holy days remind us that we're in the world but not quite of it. The authors of *Common Prayer* put words to this head-scratching idea: "We are citizens of the kingdom that transcends time, but we sojourn on a time-bound earth. Without liturgical time, we can easily forget our eternal identity."[5]

So where does that leave us?

The church year reminds us of our identity as children of God and creates a cyclical framework that holds us together through observing, honoring, and celebrating the good news of Jesus.

May the prayers in this section guide us as we explore what it means to be set apart. May they help us remember that we are not alone in our parenting. When we're bombarded by meetings and a world calling out for our family's attention 24/7, may these prayers remind us of who we are and the vibrant family of God we belong to. You'll find prayers for familiar holidays and holy days, such as New Year's, Easter, and Christmas. You'll also find a smattering of prayers for holy days that may be new to you. In addition to St. Patrick's Day and St. Valentine's Day, you'll also find the Feast Day of St. Oscar Romero and the Feast Day of St. Francis of Assisi. (For more on the liturgical calendar, see the appendix on page 205.)

These observances help us remember church history so we can raise families that look to the future in hope. It's only when we begin to understand the past, both in Scripture and in our own lives, that we begin to understand the fullness of time.

A Prayer for a New Year

January 1

O God, creator of time
And keeper of seasons,
No gods were formed before You,
Nor will there be any after You.
You hold it all,
And in You alone all things are made.

As we look at the year behind us,
Give us space to process the paths that
    got us here
So that we may have vision for what lies
    ahead.
We ask for hearts to remember
The celebrations and sorrows
Of our family's passing year.

Help us reflect on the good
Shared between us,
Of the tiny moments
Sparkling with joy,
Of the celebrations
Twinkling with hope.
May these joys
Energize us as we look to the New Year.

And help us, too, reflect on the hurts
Shared between us,
Of the small disappointments
Nestled in our hearts,

Of the mistakes
Hanging in the balance.
May these sorrows
Teach us as we look to the New Year.

As we watch time tick by
And count down to a new year,
We remember that You are a God
Of fresh starts and clean slates.
And what a gift it is
That Your mercies are new each morning
And that we don't have to wait for a
    new year
To begin again.

As we look to the New Year,
We thank You for the little ones underfoot
While the ball drops and the music starts.
Thank You for living room dance parties
With young and old
And toasts with sparkling juice,
Kisses on the forehead,
And *I love you*s.

O God, You hold all eternity in Your
    hands.
Thank You for songs to sing
And moments of quiet too.
May we reflect on the year behind us
As we look ahead to the year in front
    of us.

Isaiah 43:18-19; Lamentations 3:22-23; 2 Corinthians 5:17

A Prayer for Epiphany

January 6

We come to You, O Light in the darkness.
We come to You, O Light of the world.
We worship You, Son of God,
Whose glory has risen upon us,
Who traversed the cosmos,
And who broke into our world with love
For all people, for all places, for all time.

We have unwrapped the presents
And placed the garland back in
    the boxes.
And now, in the quiet, we seek
The brightness of Your dawn,
Just like the three kings so long ago.

Let this not be an end to Christmas joy
But rather a beginning,
Beckoning us toward the future,
Toward a life of worshiping You.

We thank You for the gifts
You have given this family—
For the laughter
And adventures shared,
For the stories,
And for the hard times
That have brought us together.

May our children reflect the imagination
    of the magi,
Living in the holy contradiction
Of the wisdom that leads
To worshiping an infant.
May our children reflect Your light.
Go with them on their journeys
In the coming years.
Guide them like a star in the sky.
Bring them to You, rejoicing
At the divine light given to us.

We come to You, O Light in the darkness.
We come to You, O Light of the world,
As we care for our children.
May we walk with them
As they enter into pilgrimages
Of their own.
May they receive the sacred gift
Of being bringers of hope
And bearers of Your great light.

Psalm 92:1-4; Isaiah 60:1, 3

A Prayer for Martin Luther King Jr. Day

Third Monday of January

O God of justice, God of truth,
We come to You on this day
To honor the life and legacy
Of Dr. Martin Luther King Jr.
And to commit our hearts
To building the beloved community
He dreamed about.

O Lord, through Dr. King,
You taught us, and are still teaching us,
What it is to stand with our oppressed
Brothers and sisters.
For whatever affects one directly
Affects all indirectly.

Lord, we thank You for Dr. King's
leadership
Against the scourge of racism
And for the ways his nonviolent teachings
Reverberate through our hearts today.
We lament the ways
We have taken his quotes out of context
And ignored the greater picture
Of his mission and ministry of social
change.

We walk in the paths Dr. King
Cleared out for us,

And yet we know many weeds
Still need to be pulled.
Help us yank the violence of racism
By the root from our hearts
And our systems.

He had a dream for his children, Lord,
And we lament the ways the dream
Is yet to be fulfilled.
Help us teach our children about
Dr. King
As a man whose work was propelled
By his love for You, Lord.
And help our children know
That this work is not over.

May our children know the cost
Of speaking out for justice and
mercy—
Friends, status, even nights in jail—
Because being obedient to Your Spirit
May scare the powerful.

Lord, help our kids know that
Speaking up against racism
And working for justice
May cost them lots of somethings,
But it will never cost their souls.

If the moral arc of the universe
Is bent toward justice,
May You ignite in our children
Flexibility and prophetic imagination
To see Your Kingdom come.

May it be so, that our earth
Reflects how it is in heaven.

Lord, the fight against racism
Starts at home.
Help our family live in mutuality,
Knowing that the good of all—
Black, indigenous, people of color—
Is tied up in our well-being,
That nobody is free
Until we all are free.
May we honor the work of Dr. King
And countless other women and men
Fighting for civil rights,
Yesterday and today,
By not shying away from the contact
     burns
It takes to keep the fires of freedom
Burning in our hearts.
For many, many tomorrows,
Lord, we pray that our parenting
And the nonviolent choices our family
     makes
With our speech, our money, our votes
Would honor our neighbor.

Protect us, Lord, from the lure of traps,
What Dr. King warned of—spiritual
     doom.
Help us remember dawn will come.
As Dr. King reminded us from the
     psalmist,
Sorrow and despair are born at night,
But morning always follows.

Let us not lose hope.
Help us do what we can
With the tools we have
To cultivate paths of peace and
     righteousness.

We honor the committed, courageous
     work
Of not only MLK
But the advocates and activists
Working tirelessly today
For a more just world for all people
In the name of Jesus Christ our Lord.

Let justice roll down like water
And righteousness like a mighty stream.
May we live as parents and children
Who enter this work with You
With urgency and sustenance from the
     Living Water,
From a well that won't run dry.

O Lord, as we honor this day,
The day of Dr. King's birth,
We lament that this nonviolent minister
Was murdered as he lived out a gospel
     of love.
May we remember and not forget
That our actions as colaborers with
     Christ, rooted in love,
Will be a threat to those who want to do
     it the old way,
Who love power and money over justice
     and humanity.

When given the choice, may our children
Know to choose community.
May they choose the love of neighbor
That flows out of the love of God—
A love that overcomes.
A love that, as Dr. King said,
Is the most durable power in the world.[6]

Amos 5:24; Ephesians 3:17; Micah 6:8

Let us not lose hope.
Help us do what we
can with the tools
we have to cultivate
paths of peace and
righteousness.

A Prayer for St. Valentine's Day

February 14

O loving God
Who never lets us down
And never lets us go,
We thank You for the gift
Of loving another.
For we know we love our spouses,
Our friends, our children
Because You have first loved us.

Lord, we pray our kids would know
Just how much they're cherished
By their earthly parents
And by the perfect love of their heavenly
    Father,
Who loves with a maternal and paternal
    spirit.
We pray our children would know us
By our love.

We pray that our children
Would know what it is to grow up
Surrounded in love,
For we can teach them lessons
And facts and figures and theories
To explain all the world,
But if we don't have love,
We are clanging cymbals,
Lost in the noise.

As we raise our children,
Help us to be patient and kind.
As we raise our children,
Help us to be humble and gentle.
As we raise our children,
Help us to be forgiving and
    compassionate.
As we raise our children,
Help us to be protective and trusting.
As we raise our children,
Help us to be hopeful and persevering.

Help us to love bravely
And to model what it is to keep choosing
    love,
Even when it's not easy—
Especially then.
May our children know the gift
Of loving another
And being loved fully in return.

We know we love imperfectly,
But we pray that Your perfect agape love
Would fill the gaps
When we fall short.
O Lord, we know that to love another
Is to be vulnerable.
And we feel it,
The way generations and generations
Of mothers and fathers have felt it
    before us—
The way our hearts drop and chests
    tighten

And we knew we were forever changed
By the glorious gift of loving another
Not because of what they can do
But simply because they are.

Lord, we know You love us with
A lavish love and glorious grace,
Not dependent on what we do
Or what we say.
Thank You for Your love
And for leading us on a path
That brings us to You.

O Lord, on this day of St. Valentine,
We come to You.
And if we pass on a legacy, Lord,
Let it be one of love
For You and for neighbor.
O Lord, let our children know us by
    our love.

———————

1 Corinthians 13; John 13:35

A Prayer for Ash Wednesday

First day of Lent

O God of dirt and dust,
We come to You on this day
Like children who know not what they do
But know they need the love of a parent
To guide them home.

We need Your mercy, O Lord,
For we are aware of the ways
We have hurt and harmed
And not honored You
With all our heart and soul,
Mind and strength.

We have been like toddlers,
Screaming when we haven't gotten our way,
Biting and hitting when we're upset.
But You welcome us
In the loving arms of Your understanding
And meet us in the humanity,
Just like a parent
Scoops up a tear-streaked, tantruming
    child
In need of rescue.

O Lord, we are so aware of our humanity,
And yet we've tried to hide it,
Covering our bruised and bloodied hearts
With self-reliance
And self-sufficiency,

Covering ourselves with
The leaves of false confidence.
But Lord, under it all,
As we raise our families
And lie awake wondering
What will become of them
And of us,
We sense our need for mercy and grace,
That we may receive
Your freely given gift of salvation.

O Lord, we like to think we're superhuman
In our parenting, in our work, in our lives.
But on this day,
We come to You
With buckling knees and blistered feet,
Weary from the journey of self.

We do not readily submit to You, Lord,
And the reminder of our own mortality is
Uncomfortable at best and painful at worst.

But we desire to raise our children
In Christ's abiding love,
And we know that for our faith
To hold water,
It must be big enough to hold even our
    suffering,
Even our death.

O God of everlasting life,
We confess to You the ways we have not
    served
As Christ served us,

And we have not forgiven
As Christ forgave us.
We take down all human posturing
To be perfect
And cast off all projections
Of seeming better than we are.
We come to You weary of the work
To always put our best foot forward
At home or at work or at church.
And instead we stumble at the foot of
    the cross
And humbly submit with honesty
The ways we have failed
To love, to serve, to forgive.

O Lord, as we mark this day,
We ask that You would cleanse our hearts.

Free us from our past
And prepare us for the future.

Thank You for Your infinite love
That knows no limits,
That gently guides us and has
    compassion
For the ways we are like little children.

Merciful God, You know the depths of
    our humanity
And lavish the knowing love
And understanding of a parent.
Thank You for being faithful to me
And for cleansing my heart again and
    again

So that I may raise my children
To know the depths of what it is to be
Fully aware of their humanity
And fully known and held
By Your forgiveness and faithfulness.

Help us not hide from our humanity.
Instead, remind us that we are but dust
And to dust we will return.
Amen.

Matthew 6:19-21; Ecclesiastes 3:20

A Prayer for Lent

The season leading up to Easter

O Lord, we come to You,
Aware that we have busied ourselves and
    our family
With full schedules brimming
With places to go
And people to see.
But in doing so,
We have forgotten You
And Your love
And the mission You have breathed into
    our lives.

We have chosen the way
Of instant gratification
And of avoidance,
Choosing an abundance of distraction
Over a reliance on You.

O Lord, we come to You,
Unsure of how to best observe Lent.
But even in our unsteady footing,
We come to You,
Arms trembling with the weight
We have taken on—
Weight that was never ours to hold.
O Lord, we want more than this for
    our kids,
And we thank You that it's never too
    late
For us to reorient our hearts to You.

O Lord, we examine our hearts—
Every worry,
Every shortcoming,
Every harbored animosity,
Every selfish act,
Every judgment.

Help us not to pick at our scabs,
But help us rip off the bandage
So that our wounds may heal, O Lord.
Shape our hearts
And the hearts of our children
To look like Yours, O God.

Our culture has beckoned us with shiny
    objects
And faster internet speed,
And we've grown accustomed to more
Instead of a daily repentance to—
And reliance on—You.
Help us know what to let go of
And what holy habits to seek.
Help us hunger and thirst for Your
    Kingdom.
May we teach our children what it is to
    go without.

We humbly admit the ways we need You,
And the ways are many, O Lord.
Help us resist temptation
And ignite in our family new ways
To join You in acts of mercy and love
To those around us,
In our communities and our streets.

Illuminate the way, O Lord,
For the paths are rocky and the sky is dark.
Illuminate in us
Our need for Your great light.
And may You shine upon our family's
    faces
So that our children
Follow Your everlasting light,
For You are the way.

During this season of Lent, O Lord,
We turn away from the ways of this world
And the lies of the evil one.
We put ourselves and our children into
    Your hands
And follow You,
The One who leads from death into life.

Philippians 3:10-11; Isaiah 58:6-7; Mark 1:12-15

Illuminate the way,
O Lord, for the
paths are rocky
and the sky is dark.
Illuminate in us
our need for
Your great light.

A Prayer for Palm Sunday

The Sunday before Easter

O Jesus, who rode in on a donkey,
Subverting again
Our ways of the world,
May we forever praise Your name
As our children wave palm branches
To welcome You in—
A parade of chubby hands
Gripping branches,
A chorus of little voices giggling,
A procession of tiny feet skipping,
Welcoming us to say, "Hosanna!
Blessed is the One
Who comes in the name of the Lord!"

We give You all the glory
And all the honor,
And we praise Your name
With the joy of a little child
Eager to join a parade,
Excited to catch the eye of Mom
    or Dad
As they make their way in worship.

Let us lift our lives in praise to You.
Let us sing unashamed, like children,
Throwing off the insecurities
That come with age
And laying them at Your feet.

Let our lives be anthems of Your love
As we enter the chorus
Of all who have gone before us,
Lifting the works of our hands
And the words of our hearts
To You, O Lord.

Enter our hearts and home.
Enter our family and our very lives,
O Lord, even as we praise You.
We know we are capable
Of the unimaginable,
And we sit in the tension
Of what is to come.

Will You prepare our hearts, O Lord,
And the hearts of our children
To remember
That these branches we hold,
The ones we cut down,
Will be made into ashes?
Will You remind us that a life in You
Is a life that holds rhythms
Of jubilant celebration
And also sorrow and suffering?

O Lord, there is none but You.
We worship You on this day
And forevermore.

Matthew 21:8-9; Psalm 118

A Prayer for Maundy Thursday

The Thursday before Easter

O Lord Jesus, who showed us love
In life and death,
Thank You for welcoming us
To Your table.

As we think about the Last Supper
You had with those dear and beloved
To You,
We are reminded of love
And life
Poured out.

We think of the final meals
We ourselves have had with loved ones
And wonder what it would be like
To say goodbye to our children,
To know our time on earth was ending,
To bring our babies close
And stroke their hair
And lift their cheeks
And say, "All of this
Was for you."
We wonder what it would be like
To say,
"Little ones, I have loved you
And I have taught you.
Remember the birthday parties
And first days of school?

Remember the holiday meals
And the walks outside?
Remember when we were together?
I will be with you
As you do all of these things again."

O Jesus, You promised Your disciples
    this—
That though Your physical body
Would soon be gone
And even betrayed
For pieces of silver,
You would leave Your presence with them
And indeed with us, Your church,
In the breaking of bread,
In the sharing of wine,
Present each time.
We serve one another in love.

O Lamb of God,
We remember You.
Help us remember
What You've called our family to:
Humility,
Service,
Sacrifice.
We are thankful.
Help us give thanks in all circumstances.

We pray that our family—
Our children and ourselves—
Would be rooted and established
In Your great love.

Help us humble ourselves in Your name.
You, Lord Jesus,
Who welcomed all to the table
And washed the dirty feet,
Sit with us in the tension of this day.
Be with us like You were in the upper
    room—
In the love
And in the fear
And even in the impending grief.

We know a light is coming,
But for now we sit in the darkness
And ask You to sit with us.
For we are broken
And also beloved.[7]

_____
Mark 14:22-24; John 13:1-17

A Prayer for Good Friday

The Friday before Easter

O Lord, we come to You on this day
To remember You—
You, who hung each star in the sky
And, too, hung upon the cross.

O Lord, we grieve and lament
And repent of the ways we have shouted,
"Crucify Him!"
With our actions and our words
And our sins of omission and silence.
Christ, have mercy on us.

O Lord, we want to skip ahead
To Your resurrection,
For it is painful
To remember Your pain—
The torture,
The death at the hands of people
    in power,
The sacrifice of Your great love.
We want to turn away.
We want the storybook ending
Without any of the sorrows.

And yet it is because of Your power
And Your suffering
That we are able to dwell in a faith
Big enough to hold all the pain of the
    world.

And we can sit in the tension
Of now and not yet.

Lord, we thank You for a love that is
    bigger
And truer than any fairy tale,
A love that bore a violent death
So that we may truly live
And be free from the shackles of violence
And the snare of power.

O Lord, our lives are marked with
    suffering,
And we do our children no favors
To present the idea that grief does not exist.
We ask You to help us
On this Friday
To create a sacred space,
To show them that You,
King of heaven and earth,
Took on our pain.
And even though You were betrayed,
Mocked, maligned, mistreated,
And even murdered,
You humbled Yourself to death on a cross
So that we would know life.
O Lord, we remember Your
Trial and torture.

We pray that our children
Would know Your way of love—
A love that makes a way
For all people,
That takes up the cross.

154

May they know a way that chooses mercy
When faced with an enemy,
A way that chooses
Sacrifice instead of comfort,
A way that chooses
Healing instead of violence,
A way that chooses
Loud love instead of hidden hate,
A way that opens their hearts
Instead of closes them shut.

O God, we ask You to hold our family
As we try to fathom love
That sacrificed on our behalf,
Willing to be betrayed
And suffer death on a cross.
Still our hearts.
Let us cry as we begin to feel
The weight of this truth.

We weep for the ways violence
Still happens in our world,
And we pray for all to know
The deep and abiding love of Jesus Christ.

We wait in the darkness.
Be with us in the darkness,
O Light of the world.

John 19:1-37; John 3:16-17; Isaiah 53:4-5; Philippians 2:7-8;
Genesis 22:1-18; Psalm 22:1-2, 9-11

A Prayer for Holy Saturday

The Saturday before Easter

O Lord, we rest in our humanity
And give thanks for the family
You have given us
As we sit together in this life.

We wait in the silence,
In the stillness,
And wonder where You are
In the quiet wanderings
Of our souls.

Today we remember Your burial
And sit in the mystery.
We marvel at how You made a way
When all seemed lost.
Today we remember those who cared
    for You—
The women and men
Who tended to Your earthly body—
And we thank You for the ways
You have created us
To care for one another
With tenderness
And great compassion.

We pray for our children, Lord.
On this day we once again

Reflect on our humanity—
On the frailty of life,
On the mystery of Your love,
On the great mutuality of
Journeying through life together.

Take this simple prayer
As we pray for our children.
May they hold space for sorrow
As well as hope.
May they hold space for pain
As well as healing.

Lord, may they know You
And seek You.
Lord, may they know Your time
Is not our time,
And in the fears of
What now? and *How can we go on?*
May they know You are near.

O Lord, may our children
Begin to fathom a love
Not bound by earth's constraints
Of time and space.
May they feel Your presence
In the waiting.
May their lives on this planet
Be surrounded by those who love
    them.
May they sense You in the unknowing.
May they know Your love
Traverses all things.

Help us hold on to the promise
That You are good,
That You are who You say You are,
Even when we can't see You,
Even when we don't know
What tomorrow brings.

———————————

Lamentations 3:1-9, 19-24; Psalm 31:1-4, 15-16

O Lord, may our
children begin to
fathom a love not
bound by earth's
constraints of
time and space.

A Prayer for Easter

O resurrected, risen King,
We praise You on this Easter morning
With glad and grateful hearts,
Eager to shout Your glory.

Death could not hold You.
Sin could not destroy You.
For You are God
And worthy of every praise!

O Jesus, You continue to make a way
Where there is no way.
As we celebrate Your resurrection power,
We pray our children
Would sing and dance
In the promise that we are Easter people
And we have a living hope in You.

May our children
Bask in the truth
That You have conquered sin and death,
And may that living hope
Spill into all they do, all they meet,
    all they are.

Lord, You know us by name,
And You do not forget us
Or forsake us.
May our children proclaim Your
    goodness,

And may they feel Your graciousness
Shine upon their faces
Like the spring dawn breaking through.

In the empty tomb,
We are given life—
And life abundant!
All the jelly beans and dyed eggs,
Baskets and bunnies
Pale in comparison to You.

O Prince of Peace, we celebrate on
    this day.
As we eat and gather around the table,
May we remember those who are lonely,
Those who have none to feast with
Or share their table with.
As we eat and gather around the table,
May we remember those who cannot
    afford
To fill their cupboards.
As we eat and gather around the table,
May we remember those whose lives
Have been marked by violence.
As we eat and gather around the table,
May we pray for all those who are
    unsafe
In sharing their faith.

As we go out into the world,
May our family live in a way
That proclaims the Good News—
Good news for the poor,
Good news that sets the captive free.

O God, the tomb could not hold You.
Fill our family with a love
That is shared between us
And freely given to everyone we meet.

The earth declares Your glory.
All of creation praises Your name.
And our hearts cry out, "Hallelujah!"
We praise You, O Lord,
As we throw off the sin and the shame of
    yesterday.
Let us dance in the promise of the new
    morning
Of today and tomorrow and forevermore!

Acts 10:34-43; 1 Corinthians 15:55-57; John 20:11-18; Luke 4:18

May our children
proclaim Your
goodness, and
may they feel Your
graciousness shine
upon their faces
like the spring dawn
breaking through.

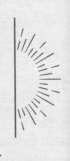

159

A Prayer for St. Patrick's Day

March 17

Christ, walk with our children.
Be present in every step and stumble.
Christ, go before our children.
Show them the way to follow in truth.
Christ, walk behind our children.
Guide them and protect them.
Christ, linger in the heart of everyone
    who thinks of our children.
May our children radiate love and
    compassion.
Christ, be on the lips of everyone who
    speaks of our children.
May our children's hearts beat with mercy,
    compassion, and truth.
Christ, be reflected in every eye that sees
    our children.
May our children show love to all they
    meet.
Christ, be in every ear that hears our
    children.
May our children sing anthems of hope
    forevermore.[8]

Psalm 96:1-7; Matthew 28:16-20; 2 Corinthians 13:14

A Prayer for the Feast Day of St. Oscar Romero

March 24

O Lord, what a humbling invitation
    it is
To raise up families for justice
And for peace.
For we know the world hates
A prophetic imagination
That says,
"In the name of Jesus, there's another
    way,
Where the last shall be first
And a lamb will lead us."

Lord, we think of Oscar Romero
And his commitment to ministry
    alongside
The oppressed and the afflicted,
The marginalized and the poor.
And on this day,
In remembrance of his life,
Taken by violence as he preached,
We reflect on how he lived up until his
    death,
Proclaiming good news for the poor
And setting the captives free,
Letting his love for You
And Your people
Overcome his fear
Of repercussions.

Lord, help us plant seeds
For Your peaceable Kingdom,
And help us water the seeds
Others have tended to before us
As we cultivate relationships with our
    children
And point them to life in You.

Choosing love is a risk,
And yet we pray that if our family
Is known,
Let us be known by our love.
If we speak, may we speak words
Of conviction,
Of truth,
Of righteousness,
And of peace.
The world is not a safe place for
    the prophet,
But may we not forget the invisible
    danger
Of staying silent
In the face of our brothers' and sisters'
    oppression,
For our flourishing
Is tied up with theirs.

Thank You for grace
To enter into hard topics
And to see beauty in the world
Even among the violence
Of word and deed.
Help us be a family
That sees ourselves as ministers,

Not messiahs.
May we proclaim a future
And indeed a reality
Created by You
And You alone.

_____

Psalm 31:15-24; John 12:20-26

May we not forget
the invisible danger
of staying silent
in the face of our
brothers' and sisters'
oppression.

A Prayer for the Annunciation

March 25

O God who makes the impossible possible,
We remember today
That You call us by name,
Much like Your angel did to Mary
So many years ago,
Intertwining God and humanity
In ways we still can barely fathom.

O God who makes the impossible
    possible,
May we go about our days,
The quiet, tucked-away moments
    of parenting,
Remembering the mystery
And the miracle
That You live in
And through us.

O God who makes the impossible possible,
We pray for our children,
That they would walk in the steps
Of the young girl so many years ago
Who courageously believed,
Who bravely trusted You.
May our children bear witness to
    Your glory
In their own lives,
With all devotion and honor and praise
    to You.

O God who makes the impossible possible,
You have done great things,
And indeed, are still doing great things
    today.
Remember Your promises of mercy
For generations to come.
And may we raise our children
So that their souls may glorify You, O Lord,
And so that their spirits may rejoice in
    You—
You, O God,
Who makes the impossible possible.

Luke 1:46-55

A Prayer for Mother's Day

Second Sunday of May

God of heaven and earth,
We feel it in our bodies and souls.
We know this to be true:
Mothers are essential.

Soft and strong,
With open arms and hearts,
We thank You for the array of
Women who are nurturing our world
In all their varied ways,
Cultivating peace
Through their mothering spirits.

We thank You for the women who
    raised us,
For the women who taught us
How to love boldly
And stand courageously.
We thank You for the women who
    showed us
How to care for others
And how to care for ourselves, too.

God of heaven and earth,
We thank You for the mothers—
The ones up late into the night,
The ones showing up and doing their best.
We thank You,
For their persistence has cared for us all.

God of heaven and earth,
We feel it in our bodies and souls.
We know this to be true:
Mothers are essential.

Isaiah 66:13; Hosea 11:3-4

A Prayer for Pentecost

Seventh Sunday after Easter

O God of mighty, rushing winds,
Would You fill our house
With Your Spirit
So we may declare Your wonders
In all we say and all we do?

O God of mighty, rushing winds,
Help our family remember
You are the God of all.
Your holy power and Your mighty
    presence
Does not belong
To just one nation or only one tongue,
To just one race or only one culture.
Forgive us, O God, for the ways we have
Believed our way is the only way,
Believed our voice is the only voice.
For in doing so, we have quenched Your
    Holy Spirit,
Sinning against You and against others.

O God of mighty, rushing winds,
Help us live with humility in Your Spirit.
Help us show our children how to stay
    curious
As part of Your church.
Light a fire in the minds and hearts
Of our daughters and sons,

So that we may be a family amazed and
    astonished
By the beauty in all who burn bright,
Wildfires of glory.
Our family is part of a global family,
Reflecting the lapping flames of Your
    love.

O God of mighty, rushing winds,
Let our home and our hearts be gathering
    places
Where borders and languages do not
    separate
Us from You or us from one another.
Ignite in our family a warmth and
    welcome
So we may always see You and feel Your
    presence
In us and in our children and in our
    neighbor.
For You have poured out Your Spirit
So liberally and so continually,
Like a wildfire that can't be contained,
Setting aglow wonders in the sky above
And embers on the earth below.

O God of mighty, rushing winds,
Would You fill our house
With Your Spirit
So we may declare Your wonders
In all we say and all we do?

Acts 2

A Prayer for Trinity Sunday

First Sunday after Pentecost

O God, blessed Trinity,
Divine mystery,
We come to You,
Reminded that You are God—
Bigger in every way,
More of everything,
More tender and more powerful,
More mighty and more merciful.

O God, blessed Trinity,
We are not left alone.
You call us beloved.
We come to You, Lord,
In awe of all we will never
Understand about Your great love.
For You are a God who dwells
In community,
In unity,
And in one and equal glory.

O God, blessed Trinity,
In all we teach our children,
In all we live ourselves,
May we honor You
In all that we are,
In all that we have.

For You are with us,
And it's in the holiest name
Of the Father, Son, and Holy Spirit
We pray.
Amen.

Psalm 8; 2 Corinthians 13:11-13; Matthew 28:16-20

A Prayer for Father's Day

Third Sunday of June

Lord, bless the fathers who swaddle babies,
Who make room in the bed after a bad
    dream,
Who cut crusts off sandwiches,
Who shout loud in the stands,
Who give advice about a job interview.
May they know the hidden moments
    are holy.

Lord, bless the fathers who never saw
    what it was
To be a nurturing dad,
Who are trying to forge a new path with
    their children,
Who keep investing with humility and
    grace.
May they know their efforts are not in vain.

Lord, bless the fathers who raised us,
Bless the daughters and sons who ache
    today.
May their hearts be comforted and healed.
And bless those who grieve the loss of
    their fathers.
May their memories provide comfort.

Lord, bless the fathers in their many forms,
Who love with open arms,
Who walk in patience and peace,

And who bring passion and playfulness
To their families, young and old.
May they feel the fullness of Your great
    love,
Today and in all days to come.

We thank You, Lord, for fathers.

Psalm 103:13; Malachi 4:6

A Prayer for the Transfiguration

August 6

O God, I believe.
Help me in my unbelief.
Bring me up to the mountain;
Flash Your brilliance like lightning
So I may understand the weight of glory,
The weight of who You are
And who I am in You.

Family life often feels
Like dancing in the dark.
We bump our shins on tables
And bang our elbows together.
We spin and we laugh;
We stumble and we fall.
We need to see You.
Illuminate the heart of this family,
For You're still opening the heavens.
The clouds still echo Your name.
You're still full of power.
Help me be still, O Lord,
So that I may see.

O God, life can feel so ordinary,
Parenting so quiet and common.
But this is a mere disguise
Because everything—everyone—
Reflects Your glory.
Remind me, O Lord,
That Jesus was no ordinary man.

And because of Your dazzling love,
We are not ordinary humans.
Help us see our children
And even ourselves, Lord,
As we truly are:
Those who radiate
Your glory.
Shine through us, Lord,
Today and forevermore.[9]

Matthew 17:1-13

Family life often
feels like dancing in
the dark. We bump
our shins on tables
and bang our elbows
together. We spin and
we laugh; we stumble
and we fall.

A Prayer on the Feast Day of St. Francis of Assisi

October 4

O God who cares for all creatures,
Big and small,
We come to You on this day
And reflect on the life of St. Francis of
    Assisi,
Who, along with so many others
In our broad lineage of faith,
Has gone before us as a living example
Of gospel transformation.

O Lord who was present in the bird's song
And the wind's breeze
Thousands of years ago
And still is today,
We ask that our children
Will choose Your paths of peace
And renounce the allure
Of what our world says brings peace—
Wealth, prosperity, prestige—
Instead choosing, like Francis,
To find You in the nature and animals
You breathed into being.

May our children be rooted in Your truth,
Not quick to float away
On the promises of a quick and easy life
When many of Your people live in poverty.
Help our children as they grow.

May they continually imagine life
Through the lens of Your gospel of peace
And Your law of love.

Give our children eyes to see the world
As You do, Lord.
Give them eyes to see You in all Your
    creation.
May our children be gentle with animals.
May they be gracious with Your land.
May they be generous with people's souls.
And like Francis, may they hold their
    worldly wealth
With open hands, willing to give it all up
For the sake of the poor and vulnerable.
May our children never lose sight
Of the Good News
Even as they see the bad.

Help us raise our children
To know that true courage
Comes not in being a savior
But in living a life
Rooted in the outstretched compassion
Of Jesus Christ, our Savior.

In the legacy of St. Francis,
May our children be peacemakers,
Walking humbling with the Lord.
May they cling to awestruck wonder
At a falling acorn.
May they see Your fingerprints
In the fluttering wings of a butterfly
And the intricate designs of a spider's web.

May our family live in service to Your
    church,
Holding on to the faith of a child
That so many of us lose,
Replacing awe of creation
With logic and reason.
We pray for humility
And for spaces in this loud world
Where our children might sit under a tree
Or rest their heads in the grass
To watch stories unfold in the shapes of
    the clouds,
To quiet their bodies and souls
To be with You.

Our world is full of noise,
And it feels so upside down to pray
For contemplative, creative spirits
In our children,
But Lord, this is what we need.

O Lord, all the animals and plants
And skies and seas
Reveal Your glory
Above us and below us and among us;
Show us Your handiwork.
Thank You for women and men of faith
Like St. Francis,
For their lives lived long ago
Remind us to walk with our family
Along Your ways.

_____

Psalm 121; Galatians 6:1-18

A Prayer for All Saints' Day

November 1

O God who holds all time and trials,
All saints and all souls
In the palm of Your hand,
We thank You for the great cloud of
    witnesses
That goes before us.

Thank You that You have not abandoned
    our family
But have surrounded us by a great body
    of believers.
We know we do not enter or depart this
    world alone
But in the lineage of many—
Those we hold dear
And those we've heard stories of
And those who walked the earth
So much earlier than us
That we can only dream up who they
    might have been.

We thank You for the women and men
Of faith who went before us,
Who lived real-life struggles
And made real-life mistakes,
For their fingerprints on our world
Have much to teach us.

We thank You for the women and men
Of faith who went before us,
Who refused to give up on You, Lord,
Who walked ways that followed Jesus.

We imagine what it would be like
To meet them someday.
We turn all the questions we might ask
Over and over in our hearts.
We think of how we might run barefoot
On heaven's path,
Welcomed into a Kingdom
Full of kin,
Through bloodlines and through
    adoption,
Ready to welcome us home.

For all the souls who have left this world,
For all those of great faith who sacrificed
    much,
We thank You for their examples
That show us which paths to take
And which to leave covered in brambles.

We pray that our sons and daughters
    would know
That no matter where life takes them,
They are never alone.
Your Spirit dwells within and among
    them,
And they have a great cloud of witnesses
That go before them.

By faith, help us show our children
What it is to run the race marked out
    for us.
Help us not lose heart.
Help us not grow weary.
By faith, help us walk
Like faithful generations before us,
Spanning dusty centuries and ancient
    ancestors,
Times and places.
May we know that faith
Is the confidence in what we hope for
And the assurance of what we do not see.

We wonder about all who prayed for
    this—
Right here where we are.
Help us teach our children
That they are welcomed into faith,
Brought here by the victories and defeats
Of the women and men before us—
That we get lifted on their shoulders
And by their prayers, too.

Hebrews 11:1–12:3

We pray that our
sons and daughters
would know that no
matter where life
takes them, they
are never alone.

A Prayer for Christ the King Sunday

Final Sunday before Advent

O Lord, we are a family crying out
For Your Kingdom to come.
You alone are God.
May Your name be praised.

Lord, our world is bleeding out,
Wounded by entrapments
Of power,
Captured by entanglements
Of the soul.

O Lord, we are a family crying out
For You on the throne,
O Prince of Peace.
You have ushered in a new Kingdom
That begins in our hearts
And grows into our world out of our souls.

O Lord, our world is bleeding out.
Help us remember that before nation
    or name,
Our identity lies in You—
You, who heal the brokenhearted,
You, who bind up our wounds.

O Lord, we are a family crying out.
Forgive us for the ways
Shiny objects have distracted us

From Your cross.
We give to You
The idols we've worshiped
As cheap replacements
For Your splendor
And Your glory
And Your wonder.

O Lord, we are a world crying out
Not just in our lack
But also in our joy—
The profound light
That comes
From the beauty
Of being in Your Kingdom.

Ephesians 1:15-23; Matthew 25:31-46

A Prayer for Advent

The season leading up to Christmas

O come, Emmanuel.
We enter this time of Advent
With holy anticipation.
We enter this sacred season
With bated breath.

O come, Emmanuel.
We're prone to get tangled
In sparkling lights and glittering tinsel,
Lost in to-do lists,
Swallowed in the seas
Of ribbons and restless hearts and
    weary souls.

O come, Emmanuel.
Our nights have not been silent,
Calm, or bright.
We have been up late
Squinting at the stars,
Trying to make sense
Of the hurting world our children will
    inherit,
And our weary hearts in it all.

O come, Emmanuel.
We see the wonder etched in our
    children's eyes,
And we ask for our grown-up anxieties
To be set free

As we await the day
To celebrate
The God who made a way.

O come, Emmanuel.
Ignite in us the awe of a child,
Looking into a manger scene
As we wait on the promise
Of the coming infant King
In a humble stable.

O come, Emmanuel.
The whole world waits for You.
We are at war with each other
And ourselves.
We have clung to our idols
Of power and pocketbooks,
And we cry out for the ways
We have reflected King Herod,
Even as we ache for You,
Prince of Peace.

O come, Emmanuel.
Help us light the candles
And illuminate the darkness
Within us.
O Light of the world,
Be with us as we recite these stories
With our children—
Of shepherds and angels and
Peace for all people.
Ring the bells
Of righteousness, of justice, of hope.

O come, Emmanuel.
Help us prepare the way
In our hearts and in our home,
In our family and in our children.
As we hang stockings and ornaments,
As we frost cookies and tie bows,
We know Your peace
Can't be bought or packaged.

O come, Emmanuel.
We anticipate great news
That we so desperately need.
Break into this world
Again and again and again,
Like You did so many years ago.
Bring joy to the people,
Hope to the hopeless,
Light to the darkness.
And may we and our children
Prepare You room
So that we may be instruments
Of Your peace.

O come, Emmanuel.
We thank You for this time of
    anticipation
And for the glimmers of Your light
Spilling in even now
Among the ornaments and the candy
    canes.
We thank You for this time of together.
Help us to get quiet, to get small
So we can make space in our souls

For the Newborn
Who will illuminate the darkness
And change everything.

O come,
O come,
Emmanuel.

_____

John 1:3-5

A Prayer for the Feast Day of St. Nicholas

December 6

As we hang stockings or set out shoes,
We anticipate Your arrival, O Lord.
In these times
Of great darkness in our world
And division in our land,
We ache for You
And wonder if the small ways we love
Can really make a difference.

We thank You for St. Nicholas of Myra,
Whom we celebrate on this day.
We rejoice over a life lived so long ago
Out of great love for You.
We pray that we will be like St. Nicholas,
Whose devotion to You
Is seen in the stories of his quiet love
    for those
Society often deemed unworthy of being
    seen—
The children and the laborers
And those struggling to make ends meet.
We ask that we would be parents who
Cultivate goodness and generosity
In our children
Out of their love for You, O God.

In the paths of St. Nicholas,
Who sold his possessions

And gave his inheritance
To those on the margins,
Help our family love
The sick and the suffering
Out of a love that pours out of
Your everlasting love.

We thank You for this Christlike model
Of a compassionate life—
Of ransoms secretly paid,
Of warmth on a cold day—
And we find great hope and great joy
In honoring his life of faith.

O Lord, guard us against
Our possessions possessing us.
Our world whispers
That we should buy more,
That Christmas memories will only be
    as good
As the gifts under the tree.
But we know there's a more beautiful way,
Where we give what we can
Out of our hearts,
Needing nothing in return
And finding great hope in You.

Help us be like St. Nicholas,
Who saw those who suffered
And was moved to make bold changes
    in his life
So those around him could simply live.

O God, we know radical hospitality
Is needed in our world.

And yet life in Your upside-down
    Kingdom
Pushes against the norms of our nations,
Which equate flourishing with 401(k)s.
And on this day, we reflect on how
St. Nicholas's Kingdom living
Made those in charge—
The power brokers of his time—
Feel so threatened that they exiled him.

O God, even as we celebrate
With candies and stockings and tiny
    shoes,
We know that a life lived in radical love,
A life that honors God and neighbor
Above all else,
Led St. Nicholas to a life of
Suffering, imprisonment, and exile.
May we be brave enough to give
A little more love on this day.
May we be brave enough
To remember that while history
May revere and honor those who,
Like Nicholas, followed You,
Even when it meant subverting
The ways of the world,
Not everyone appreciates acts
Of goodness and generosity
Toward the most forgotten
And oppressed among us.

O God, remind us that You are a friend
To those in need,
A protector of weary hearts

And worn-out bodies,
A helper to all who need it.
Help us raise our family
With this kind of noticing love.
Lord, we thank You, too,
For Nicholas's parents,
Who raised him to know Your love
And the peace of Your Kingdom,
Even when he was a young child.
May their model inspire our parenting.
Let our children know Your love,
For if a time comes when we are not
    together,
As it happened with Nicholas's family,
Their love for You will direct their paths.

Help us honor the love
You have whispered in our hearts
By raising our children to work
For peace on earth.
In every tradition and celebration,
May we remember who You are.
Give us imagination to see You
In those that many choose to turn
    away from.
For in the turning toward,
We welcome You, O Lord.

1 John 4:7-14; Psalm 78:3-7; Mark 10:13-16

PRAYER TO PRAY WITH CHILDREN

God, thank You for Your real and true
    and good love.
Thank You for St. Nicholas, who lived
    so long ago.
Will You help us be generous like him?
And when we look at our stockings hanging
Or our shoes at the door,
Will You remind us that we can see You
    in our neighbors?
God, in this Advent season,
Remind us that the biggest joy doesn't
    come in presents
But in the gift of being loved and getting
    to give our love away too.

A Prayer for Christmas Morning

December 25

O Christ Jesus, joy of the world,
We celebrate Your arrival—
Word made flesh—
On this Christmas morn.

O God incarnate,
As we celebrate and watch our children
Squeal with delight
With sleepy eyes and tousled hair
Or grin in spite of themselves,
May we wonder what Mary felt
As she watched her baby grow.
We know we are in but a flash in time.
We want to hold these moments.
We want to store them up in our hearts.
And as we watch our children,
Warm with last night's sleep,
We marvel that You,
Maker of heaven and earth,
Entered this world as one of us—
A cosmic King made vulnerable infant,
Swaddled in strips of cloth—
And You let us hold You in our arms.

O Prince of Peace,
In our celebrations and rejoicing,
We watch the light break in,
And we pray, too, for those who are
Alone this morning,

Who ache for the gift of together
And spend the day in quiet—
No melodies of little voices,
No choruses of laughter at the table.
Comfort the lonely, and bring joy to the
    hurting.
Fill the hungry, and lift the lowly.
And may we know, O Redeemer,
That this work of peace on earth
Begins in us.

O Spirit of the living God,
As our children pull presents
From under the tree,
We know these paper boxes
Are but temporary joys
In the light of Your glory.
We thank You for the good gift
Of Jesus,
And we thank You that
You have given and still offer now
Gifts of love and joy,
Of peace and patience,
Gifts of kindness and goodness,
Of faithfulness and self-control.

O God of mercy,
We rejoice, for on this morning
We celebrate the day of Christ's arrival—
The day that changed everything.
And we give all the glory to You
Forevermore.

Luke 1:46-55

180

May we know,
O Redeemer,
that this work of
peace on earth
begins in us.

PART EIGHT

Breath Prayers

BREATH PRAYERS ARE short meditations to help you focus your body and mind on the One who gives each breath. Rooted in Scripture, these simple praises and petitions act as connection points, providing space to slow your breathing and be present with God.

The contemplative practice of praying as you inhale and exhale has been used by Christians for generations as a way to be still and know that God is God (see Psalm 46:10). Breath prayer is simply an invitation to take a moment to breathe and center your thoughts on the reality of the Creator, who dwells in you and among you always.

As you inhale and exhale deeply, ask God to help you become mindful of your breath and your body. In our overwhelming daily realities, it's easy to become disconnected from who God has created us to be—fully human, with a connected heart, soul, mind, and body (see Luke 10:27). If parenting is a continual undoing, these breath prayers act as a tangible invitation to let God piece us back together, breath by breath.

You can say these prayers silently or repeat the words aloud. Whether you're rocking a baby, helping with homework, or stuck in traffic, integrate these mindful moments into the rhythms of your day. Many of the prayers are easy to memorize or pray with your children too. Close your eyes (unless you're driving, of course!) and settle your body. There's no right or wrong way to do this. Maybe you'll find that you like resting a hand on your heart or stomach as you say the words—or maybe it works for you to pray to yourself as you go on a walk. You might repeat the prayers every morning or at the end of the day before turning off the light.

Whatever your circumstances, you can integrate these simple phrases into the rhythms of your day. Pray them at any time or in any place. The God of all things is already there.

For When You're Tired

INHALE: I'm weary.

EXHALE: You give me rest.

Use this short prayer to check in on how you're doing. How is your mind? Your body? Your soul? In Matthew 11:28, Jesus welcomes the weary and the burdened, offering to give rest. Give yourself a minute (or as long as you need) to stop to let your breath become a prayer, accepting Jesus' offer for divine soul rest.

For When You Need to Feel God's Love

INHALE: Nothing can separate

EXHALE: Me from Your love.

When we participate in breath prayers, we center our bodies and souls into the truth of God's love. Inhale; exhale. Do it once or as many times as you need. This is also a simple one to pray with your kids. It's taken from Romans 8:39.

For When You Need Direction

INHALE: Guide me, O God.

EXHALE: My hope is in You.

Breath prayers help us center on the truth of who God is and who we are—mind, body, and soul. Breathe in; breathe out. Release your shoulders as you release your worries to the One who holds it all. May this breath prayer from Psalm 25:5 remind you to cling to hope.

For When You Feel Alone

INHALE: You won't fail me

EXHALE: Or abandon me.

Inhale and exhale God's promise. People, places, and policies will disappoint. But God will not fail or abandon you, just as God has never failed or abandoned God's people. This breath prayer is from Joshua 1:5. May you feel stronger and more courageous as you breathe in and out the promise that God will not disappoint, even when others do.

For When Life Feels Chaotic

INHALE: My heart seeks You.

EXHALE: Don't let me stray.

Feel your heartbeat. Remember God is near. Rest in the truth that you—and your kids—are known and held in the chaos. This is from Psalm 119:10.

For When You Need Peace

INHALE: Hear my cry, Lord.

EXHALE: Listen to my cries for mercy.

May this breath prayer bring a moment of peace as you ask God for mercy to fill your heart and your world. Breathe in; breathe out. Take a few minutes to pause from the scroll and pray. This prayer is taken directly from Psalm 86:6.

Rest in the truth that you— and your kids—are known and held in the chaos.

For When You're Afraid

INHALE: I see You in the wind and the waves.

EXHALE: I won't be afraid.

A breath prayer for when the strong winds blow and the waters grow rough. Inhale the presence of Jesus; exhale lingering fears. Take as long as you need to stop, breathe, and pray. This breath prayer is inspired by John 6:16-21.

For When You Need to Be Reminded of God's Character

INHALE: You're good, O Lord.

EXHALE: Your love endures forever.

This prayer is a reminder to release your shoulders and breathe. Inhale God's goodness, and breathe out God's love. Even in the most challenging times, God is still good. And God's love never fails. What a great mystery and comfort this is. This breath prayer is from Psalm 106:1.

For When You Feel Weak

INHALE: Your grace is enough.

EXHALE: I don't have to be strong.

Breathe in the grace of God; breathe out every feeling of needing to be strong. Let your breath become prayer. This breath prayer is from 2 Corinthians 12:9: "My grace is sufficient for you, for my power is made perfect in weakness."

For When You Need Hope

INHALE: I put my hope in You.

EXHALE: Help me travel along Your paths.

Take a minute to inhale hope and exhale God's presence on your path. May this breath prayer from Psalm 37:34 remind you that you are not without hope, even as you look to the future and wonder what your children's paths might look like.

For When You Need to Guard Your Tongue

INHALE: May my words and my heart

EXHALE: Be pleasing to You, O God.

Take a minute to breathe in and breathe out. May your words and the very meditations of your heart be pleasing to the Lord, your Rock and Redeemer. This prayer is from Psalm 19:14.

For When You Need to Remember Who's in Control

INHALE: All has been created through You.

EXHALE: All has been created for You.

Breathe in; breathe out. As you center on this breath prayer, let it help you reflect on the love of God in you and among you, and let your body rest in our Creator God, who through Christ created all things visible and invisible, all things seen and unseen. This breath prayer is from Colossians 1:16.

You are not without hope, even as you look to the future and wonder what your children's paths might look like.

For When You Need Forgiveness

INHALE: Create in me a clean heart, O God.

EXHALE: Renew my spirit within me.

As you breathe in and out, focus on God's steadfast mercy. It's never too late to begin again. This breath prayer comes from Psalm 51:10.

For When Your Heart Is Heavy

INHALE: O God, I ache for answers.

EXHALE: Let me see Your goodness.

On your inhale, acknowledge what is heavy on your soul. On your exhale, remember God's goodness, love, and mercy. This breath prayer is from Psalm 69:16.

For When You Don't Know What to Do

INHALE: Teach me Your ways

EXHALE: So I may walk in Your paths.

Inhale; exhale. Remember that this journey is about taking each next step of faith, not having all the answers. This is from Micah 4:2.

For When You Are Waiting on God

INHALE: I will be still.

EXHALE: Help me wait for You.

Breathe in the peace of God; breathe out the patience of the Spirit. Take a minute to let this breath prayer from Psalm 37:7 help settle your anxieties.

For When You Feel Burned Out

INHALE: I will stay in Your company.

EXHALE: Help me learn to live freely and lightly.

This is a breath prayer for when you feel tired, worn out, or maybe even burned out on religion. Breathe in; breathe out. May this centering prayer help you learn the unforced rhythms of grace as you care for your children. This meditation is from Matthew 11:28-30: "Are you tired? Worn out? Burned out on religion? Come to me. Get away with me and you'll recover your life. I'll show you how to take a real rest. Walk with me and work with me—watch how I do it. Learn the unforced rhythms of grace. I won't lay anything heavy or ill-fitting on you. Keep company with me and you'll learn to live freely and lightly" (MSG).

For When You Are Weary

INHALE: Help me to act justly and love mercy.

EXHALE: Help me not grow weary as I walk with You.

Breathe in God's heart for justice and mercy. Breathe out God's promise to walk with you. As weary as you may feel, let your spirit rest and be renewed as you pray this breath prayer from Micah 6:8. Your efforts for a more just and merciful world for your children are not in vain—they mirror what God asks of us in our walk.

For When You Are Worried

INHALE: Help me focus on today.

EXHALE: I won't worry about tomorrow.

Breathe in the realities of today; breathe out the worries of tomorrow. It's easy to feel anxious about the world our kids are inheriting. May the Lord take our anxieties about what we can't control tomorrow and use them to spur us into action for the things we can do today. This breath prayer is inspired by Matthew 6:34.

For When You Feel like You Can't Go On

INHALE: O God, I can do this.

EXHALE: You give me strength.

Breathe in and breathe out this simple prayer inspired by Philippians 4:13. We can stand firm in justice and in truth because the God of peace is with us.

For When Your Mind Is Swirling

INHALE: You are tender and merciful.

EXHALE: Guide me to the path of peace.

This breath prayer is an invitation to breathe in God's tender mercy and breathe out your assurance in God's guidance. This prayer is inspired by Luke 1:78-79.

For When You Are Ready to Give Up

INHALE: I won't lose heart.

EXHALE: You are renewing me.

Take a minute (or as long as you need) to pray this breath prayer. Breathe in hope for the weary; breathe out the reminder that God is making all things new. This prayer is inspired by 2 Corinthians 4:16.

For When You Want to Praise

INHALE: My soul glorifies You, O Lord,

EXHALE: And my spirit rejoices in You.

INHALE: Your mercy goes on and on.

EXHALE: You perform mighty deeds.

INHALE: You bring down rulers

EXHALE: And lift the humble.

INHALE: You fill the hungry

EXHALE: And send the rich away.

INHALE: You remember to be merciful,

EXHALE: Just like You promised.

Inhale; exhale. This breath prayer comes from the Magnificat, Mary's revolutionary song of praise in Luke 1:46-55. May we incorporate these truths into how we raise our children.

For When You Need a Reminder of Your Identity

INHALE: O Redeemer, You crown me

EXHALE: With love and compassion.

This is a breath prayer to help us center on God's compassionate love. May we hear David's psalm and remember that we don't belong to the empires of this world; instead, we wear the crown of God's upside-down Kingdom. This breath prayer is from Psalm 103:4.

For When You're on Overdrive

INHALE: My heart is glad

EXHALE: And my body can rest.

Inhale; exhale. Allow your shoulders to release and remember that you can find rest in God's love. This breath prayer is from Psalm 16:9: "My heart is glad and my tongue rejoices; my body also will rest secure."

For When You Need to Be Reminded of God's Presence

INHALE: You are with me.

EXHALE: You will never leave me.

Inhale a reminder of God's presence, and exhale God's promise to never leave you. We don't know what the future holds, but we can meditate on this truth. This is from Deuteronomy 31:6.

For When You Face Injustice

INHALE: You give strength to the weary.

EXHALE: You give power to the weak.

As you breathe in and out, pray these words from Isaiah 40:29. God sees what is unjust. God hears our lament. God weeps with us when we grieve what grieves the heart of God.

For When You Need Perspective

INHALE: I will remember Your wonders of old.

EXHALE: I will meditate on Your works.

In confusing times, may this breath prayer help your soul center on the ancient wonder of who God is and what He has done. Be still and remember. This prayer is from Psalm 77:11-12.

For When You Feel Anxious

INHALE: O God, I give You my anxieties.

EXHALE: O God, You care for me.

This breath prayer is from 1 Peter 5:7. Take a minute or two to use this meditation to help you center on God's ever-present love.

You give strength
to the weary.
You give power
to the weak.

For When You Are Discouraged

INHALE: You go before me.

EXHALE: I will not be afraid.

With every breath, give every discouragement, big and small, to the Maker of heaven and earth. This prayer is taken from Deuteronomy 31:8.

For When You Need Proof of God's Goodness

INHALE: Give me a sign of Your goodness.

EXHALE: Help me and comfort me.

We turn our anxieties to the God who does not shame us for our fears but offers arms of welcome and warmth. This breath prayer is inspired by Psalm 86:17.

For When You Walk through Complicated Times

INHALE: I know the Lord secures justice for the poor

EXHALE: And upholds the cause of the needy.

INHALE: Surely the righteous will praise Your name

EXHALE: And the upright will live in Your presence.

This is a breath prayer for complicated times, taken from Psalm 140:12-13. Inhale the Lord's tender, all-knowing ways and exhale the Lord's merciful, ever-present Spirit. With every breath, may we be reminded of Him.

For When You Are Down

INHALE: My soul is cast down within me.

EXHALE: I will remember You.

Wherever you are, name your emotions in an inhale, and then exhale God's love and divine presence. This prayer is taken from Psalm 42:6.

For When You Are Distracted

INHALE: You are my help.

EXHALE: I sing in the shadow of Your wings.

Are you distracted? Unable to find the words? Unable to find the time? The good news is that God's faithfulness doesn't depend on us. This meditation comes from Psalm 63:7.

For an Ordinary Day

INHALE: Have mercy on me.

EXHALE: Hear my prayer.

Prayer doesn't have to be complicated. Breathe in; breathe out. God hears you, sees you, and knows you—and your kids. This breath prayer is from Psalm 4:1.

For a Busy Day

INHALE: Your steadfast love surrounds me.

EXHALE: I trust in You, O Lord.

Take a minute (or as long as you need) to breathe in and breathe out this simple prayer taken from Psalm 32:10.

For a Monday Morning

INHALE: Spirit, You are with me

EXHALE: Even when there are no words.

May this Monday meditation guide you toward God's truth even as you're inundated with the demands of parenthood. This breath prayer comes from Romans 8:26, which tells us the Holy Spirit helps us in our weakness.

For the Beginning of the Week

INHALE: Let justice roll like a river

EXHALE: And righteousness like a mighty stream.

This is a breath prayer to begin your week, taken from Amos 5:24. Inhale and meditate on God's justice; exhale and meditate on God's righteousness. May this Scripture breathe life into us as we do the work of dismantling injustice in our lives and in our parenting. Here is a modern paraphrase of Amos 5:23-24: "I've had all I can take of your noisy ego-music. When was the last time you sang to *me*? Do you know what I want? I want justice—oceans of it. I want fairness—rivers of it. That's what I want. That's *all* I want" (MSG).

For the Middle of the Week

INHALE: When I am afraid,

EXHALE: I put my trust in You.

We worry for our children, for what's to come in the weeks and months ahead. But in this midweek meditation, we take a break to breathe out our fear and breathe in God's comfort from Psalm 56:3.

For When You Wake Up in the Morning

INHALE: Because of Your mercy,

EXHALE: Light is about to break.

INHALE: Illuminate the darkness.

EXHALE: Guide us to peace.

Breathe in God's tender mercy; breathe out the truth that the morning light from heaven is about to break upon us. As you breathe, remember that God gives light to you and your children, even in the darkness, and guides you on the path of peace. This is taken from Luke 1:78-79.

For the End of the Day

INHALE: Your mercies never cease.

EXHALE: Your mercies never end.

As you feel your own exhaustion at the end of the day, breathe in God's love and breathe out God's never-ending mercy. This breath prayer is inspired by Lamentations 3:22.

For Going to Sleep or Waking Up

INHALE: You are my God, who takes my hand

EXHALE: And tells me You will help me.

This is a prayer for when you rest your head at night and when you wake in the morning. Breathe in God's presence; breathe out God's care for you. As you pray, center on your belovedness. This is also an easy prayer to pray with your kids. This breath prayer is from Isaiah 41:13.

A Benediction

May all your life
Be a prayer—
A holy kiss
Atop sticky foreheads and matted
    curls.

May all your life
Be a prayer—
Learning each day afresh
What it is to see God in you
And God in your neighbor.

May all your life
Be a prayer—
An offering of presence and peace,
Poured out and replenished
Between parent and child.

May all your life—
Your fantastic,
Dirty,
Messy,
Holy
Life—
Be a prayer.

May all your life—
your fantastic, dirty,
messy, holy
life—be a prayer.

Acknowledgments

Getting out of the way and listening
is not something that comes easily,
either in art or in prayer.

MADELEINE L'ENGLE

MY DEEPEST HOPE is that this book is an outpouring of listening, an offering of paying attention. I'm grateful to every mother and father who shared their deepest joys and sorrows with me—their fingerprints and heartbeats are woven into every prayer in this book. I pray that I have held your experiences with care and honored your stories with grace. May you know how deeply grateful I am for you. You matter to God, and you matter to me.

To my parents, Scott and Regina: I am the mother I am because of the parents you are. Thank you for raising a daughter who felt like she could dream big, knowing she would always have loving arms to fall back into. For all the hours of playing pretend, all the times you hunkered into the front seat at plays and tennis meets, and all the late-night teenage drama you sat through—please know your care is appreciated in new ways as I parent my own kids now. You've given me big shoes to fill. Thanks for letting me sit on your deck to write so much of this book when my house was too noisy and for always making sure I was fed, too. Most of all, thanks for modeling unconditional, real-life parental (and now grandparental!) love. My prayers only exist because of yours. (Also: I'm sorry for the gray hairs I've given you along the way. My kids are paying me back now.)

To the dear family and friends who have shown up through the years at countless birthdays and graduations, airport arrivals and Sunday morning baptisms: your presence in my life and in the lives of my children means the world to me. Thank you. I'm especially grateful for my brother Nathan, who has set the bar ridiculously high for being an uncle. Thank you to all the great-grandparents and grandparents who have given me legacies of love. And to my in-laws: thank you for raising a son who is a true gift of grace (and a fount of comic relief) on this journey together.

To my agent, Rachelle Gardner: thank you for believing in me and this book. You have been a trusted guide in the publishing journey. To everyone on the Tyndale team: your warmth, wisdom, and welcome have been deeply felt. I extend a deep thanks to Jillian Schlossberg, who championed this book with care and creativity when it was just a baby of an idea. Thank you doesn't seem like enough, friend. To Stephanie Rische, who generously and graciously midwifed each stanza and every section: thank you for sharing your craft with me. I'm not sure every author looks forward to emails from their editor the way I have. To Eva Winters, thank you for crafting such a timeless, modern design. And to Brittany Bergman: thank you for making these pages shine.

Life does not happen in a vacuum, and I'm forever grateful for the community, grace, and encouragement the people at Meredith Drive Reformed Church showed me during the writing of this book. You know who you are.

To the book club ladies who managed to throw me a socially distanced celebratory book party in the midst of a pandemic: thank you for seeing me and for always being willing to talk late into the night about *all the things*. To the Kimballs, the Hoovers, the Karnishes, and the Whites: thanks for your genuine, honest, funny friendship—and for always being a text away. We all need sweatpants friends. Thanks for being ours. I think you're great humans, friends, and parents.

To the ladies of *Upside Down Podcast*, Lindsy, Patricia, and Alissa: What would I do without all our Voxer messages? Thank you for teaching me how to act justly, love mercy, and walk humbly with God in truly embodied ways. To Diana, Lindsey, and Jess: our group texts can actually never stop. Never, ever, ever. I just love you too much. Thank you for being exactly you and for pushing me to live into my full humanity too. To Jenn: thank you for creating a sacred space and inviting me in. What a joy.

To Eric Idehen: the way you embody the love of Christ and the way you have become a father to so many inspires me every day. Thank you for your ministry and your friendship.

To the late Mrs. Olabelle Reed, my second-grade teacher, who taught me to memorize Dr. Martin Luther King Jr.'s "I Have a Dream" speech: I still have the angel you gave me at my high school graduation, Mrs. Reed. Thank you for opening my young mind and heart to a bigger world. I pray I do the same for the next generation.

And now, to my children, Joseph, Asher, Eliza, and Abram: these prayers, as you know, have always been for you. I hope you see little bits of my heart—and little pictures of our life together—nestled into these pages. I will never have enough words for all the glorious ways you radiate God's love to me. Thank you. My life is better because of each one of you. I love you, and I love being your mom.

Jonny, I threatened to put a lot of funny things about you in the acknowledgments, but when it comes down to it, I mostly just want to say thank you. Thank you for affirming my vocation and encouraging me to write when I didn't think I could muster one more word. Thank you for parenting four young children so well all by yourself when I needed quiet to work on another paragraph. Thank you for partnering with me in all of life's ordinary and extraordinary adventures—and for modeling empathy and compassion to me daily. Thank you for being my first reader and the last one I kiss at night. Thank you for making me laugh. Thank you for being you. It's a gift to grow up and grow old together. I love you.

And to the God of all things: thank You for lighting the way.

Liturgical Calendar

WHEN OUR LIVES FEEL increasingly divided and chaotic, following the rhythms of Jesus' life keeps us rooted, reminding us that we belong to God and to each other.

Beginning at Advent, the liturgical year gives us a new way to view time, guiding us through the mystery and wonder of Jesus, and reminding us of our place in God's story. In the liturgical year, we remember who we are and the rhythms that have guided Christians throughout history.

Whether or not you attend a liturgical church or denomination, understanding time through the lens of Jesus' life roots all of us in our broader identity as believers. In the liturgical year, we have an invitation to reflect on our own spiritual journeys too.

The liturgical calendar is split into six seasons:

- **Advent:** a time of preparation for the coming Christ
- **Christmas:** a time of celebration of the birth of Jesus
- **Epiphany (Ordinary Time):** a time of observation of the life of Jesus
- **Lent:** a time of reflection on the death of Jesus
- **Easter:** a time of jubilation of the resurrection of Jesus
- **Pentecost (Ordinary Time):** a time of annunciation of the Spirit in us

The liturgical calendar invites us to reorder our time around and reorient ourselves to the life of Christ. As my friend Jenn says, "The liturgical year helps us walk through the seasons of our lives in tune with the seasons of Christ's life, growing as we go." Using the liturgical year as a guide for prayer invites us to remember that we are one body, united across time and place.

My hope is that this wheel will help you visualize this cyclical calendar, especially as you pray the prayers in part seven.

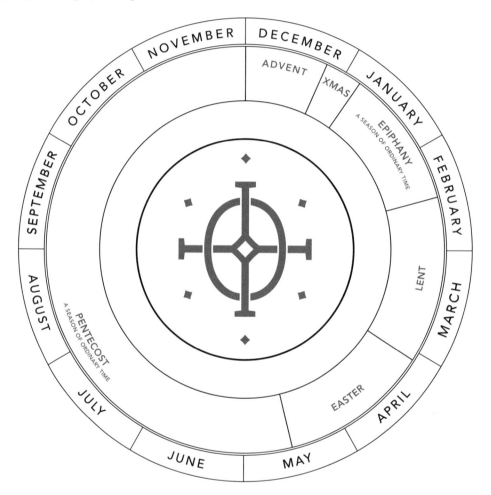

Credit: Jenn Giles Kemper, Sacred Ordinary Days

Notes

1. Pádraig Ó Tuama, *Daily Prayer with the Corrymeela Community* (London: Canterbury Press Norwich, 2017), xii.
2. Paula D'Arcy, quoted at Richard Rohr, "Negative Capability," Center for Action and Contemplation, January 11, 2016, https://cac.org/negative-capability-2016-01-11/.
3. Walter Brueggemann, *Prayers for a Privileged People* (Nashville: Abingdon Press, 2008), 1.
4. Shane Claiborne, Jonathan Wilson-Hartgrove, and Enuma Okoro, *Common Prayer: A Liturgy for Ordinary Radicals* (Grand Rapids, MI: Zondervan, 2010), 17.
5. Claiborne, Wilson-Hartgrove, and Okoro, *Common Prayer*, 17.
6. Inspired by Martin Luther King Jr., "Letter from a Birmingham Jail [King, Jr.]," April 16, 1963, Center for Africana Studies, University of Pennsylvania, https://www.africa.upenn.edu/Articles_Gen/Letter_Birmingham.html; Martin Luther King Jr., "A Knock at Midnight," June 5, 1963, Martin Luther King, Jr. Research and Education Institute, Stanford University, https://kinginstitute.stanford.edu/king-papers/documents/knock-midnight. See also Martin Luther King Jr., *"Thou, Dear God": Prayers That Open Hearts and Spirits*, ed. Lewis V. Baldwin (Boston: Beacon Press, 2012).
7. The comparison between Jesus' teachings at the Last Supper and a dying parent's final instructions were inspired by Vicki K. Black, *Welcome to the Church Year: An Introduction to the Seasons of the Episcopal Church* (Harrisburg, PA: Morehouse, 2004), 80.
8. See "I Bind unto Myself Today," words attributed to Saint Patrick, paraphrased by Cecil F. Alexander (1889), Open Hymnal Project, http://openhymnal.org/Pdf/I_Bind_Unto_Myself_Today-St_Patricks_Breastplate.pdf.
9. Inspired by C. S. Lewis, *The Weight of Glory* (New York: HarperOne, 2001); Vicki K. Black, *Welcome to the Church Year: An Introduction to the Seasons of the Episcopal Church* (Harrisburg, PA: Morehouse, 2004), 121.

Index

About the Author

KAYLA CRAIG believes in creating a more compassionate world for her four children—and for children everywhere. With a family knit together through birth and adoption, Kayla has stayed up countless nights searching for the right words to pray for her children's varied personalities and needs. She and her pastor-husband, Jonny, can often be found chasing their spirited kids (and two dogs) across their home in Iowa, leaving a trail of discarded fruit snacks wherever they go.

A former journalist, Kayla is adamant about paying attention and staying curious. Driven to listen and learn, Kayla brings her reporting background to her work as a writer and professional podcast producer. Savvy in front of a mic (and behind the scenes), Kayla cofounded and hosts the *Upside Down Podcast*, a place for ecumenical conversations on faith, justice, and God's upside-down Kingdom. Professionally, she writes, produces, and edits prayers and podcasts for Christian spiritual formation.

When she's not producing podcasts, playing LEGOs with her boys, or advocating for her disabled daughter, Kayla writes about parenting, peacemaking, and prayer. Her most recent published essays are in *This Is Motherhood: A Motherly Collection of Reflections + Practices* (Sounds True, 2019) and *Rally: Communal Prayers for Lovers of Jesus and Justice* (Fresh Air Books, 2020). She is a regular writer for PBS KIDS for Parents.

Kayla weaves stories that cross divides and sow love instead of hate. You can find her making space for "just one more" old book on the shelf or adding "just one more" new friend to the table. She has a penchant for deep mugs of coffee, deeper belly laughs, and even deeper questions. You can connect with Kayla at kaylacraig.com and on Instagram @kayla_craig and @liturgiesforparents.